The Big Book of
Comprehension Capers

Main Ideas
Inferences

Grades 1–6

L. D. Ceaser

Fearon Teacher Aids
a division of
David S. Lake Publishers
Belmont, California

The Big Book of Comprehension Capers brings you over two hundred completely reproducible blackline masters. You'll be able to present endless combinations of creative activities and engage your students in critical reading and thinking.

Use the table of contents on the next page to find the list of sections in this book. Each section is identified by a handy tab. For a complete list of the activities in any of the four sections, simply use the appropriate tab as designated by the table of contents. Also, you'll be glad to note the introductory information in each section because there are suggestions that will help you plan further instructional sequences to help students read critically.

Editorial director: Ina Tabibian
Development editor: Maureen E. Hay
Managing editor: Emily Hutchinson
Production editor: Stephen Feinstein
Design director: Eleanor Mennick
Designer: Colleen Forbes
Illustrator: Duane Bibby
Compositor: Pamela Cattich
Manufacturing director: Casimira Kostecki

ISBN 0-8224-1479-1

Printed in the United States of America
1. 9 8 7 6 5 4 3 2 1

Contents

Part I

Main Ideas

Main Idea Maneuvers

Grades 1–3

Contents

Introduction

The lessons in this workbook develop eight subskills for determining main idea. The worksheets are organized by section, each section focusing on one of the eight subskills.

1. **Identifying Repetition and Redundancy**
2. **Determining Relevance**
3. **Classifying Nouns**
4. **Classifying Series of Events**
5. **Identifying Topic Sentences**
6. **Inventing Topic Sentences**
7. **Identifying Main Idea**
8. **Understanding and Using Titles**

At the conclusion of each activity is an evaluation code box.

◯ = too easy	▢ = too hard	△ = just right

An evaluation of item difficulty can be made by enclosing the item number within one of the shapes shown in the box to relay the coded message. Another way to use the code box is simply to shade in the shape that best evaluates the page. This evaluation might be made by the teacher, the student, a tutor, or a team. The code is designed to help determine skill areas needing further attention.

The following section suggests additional activities for continued practice in the subskills necessary for identifying main ideas and in understanding and using titles.

Additional Activities

1. Classifying

Help students categorize nouns and verbs. Have them play "Twenty Questions" with categories. Here are some examples of categories you might wish to use:

kinds of weather	temperature words
types of homes	names of games
names of colors	television shows
ways to feel	titles of books
types of dogs	location words
names of tools	types of food
classroom tools	names of cars

Follow this procedure for "Twenty Questions":
- Choose a student to be "It."
- Have "It" think of an item in any category and say, for example, "I am thinking of a title."
- Have other students, in turn, ask questions that can be answered "Yes" or "No."
- The winner is the person who can guess the item before twenty "No" answers have been given.
- The winner can be the next "It." If no one guesses the item, the original "It" can go again.

2. Vocabulary

Vocabulary activities provide useful practice in thinking and deciding which are parts of the process of determining main ideas. Crossword puzzles, activities using synonyms and homonyms, and root word lessons are all beneficial. For example, have students try to make new words by using known prefixes and suffixes.

dis- (opposite)	-able (able)
un- (not)	-ing (in process)
in- (not)	-s (plural)
re- (again)	-ed (past)
non- (none)	-est (most)

3. Scrambled Words

Write scrambled words on the board. Tell students the category the words are in, and ask them to unscramble the words. Here are some examples:

oatts, pplae, nnaaba: things we eat (toast, apple, banana)

nur, kwal, pjmu: ways we move (run, walk, jump)

4. Poetry

Have students write the letters of their names vertically on a sheet of paper. Then have them use each letter to begin a line of a poem. Have them tell about themselves. Here is an example:

Likes to read
Is funny sometimes
Zips through chocolate cake

5. Comparisons

Have students compare themselves with their parents. Have them tell how they are alike and how they are different. Then have them compare two classrooms, two teachers, two games, two pets, two hobbies, two friends, and so on.

6. Crossword Puzzles

Have students write down interesting words from a story or book and define the terms in the context of the story. Then have them use the words to make a crossword puzzle. Here is an example:

Henry = main character
ran = how he got home

7. Word Associations

Have students write a list of words associated with a given topic. Then have them read their words aloud. Discuss how the words are related. Here is an example:

Winter—cold, snow, ice, snowman, snowballs, snowsuits, sweaters, mittens, scarves, hats, sleds, hills

8. Add-Ons

Name an object and direct the students to draw a picture of it. Continue to name additional objects for the students to draw. Here is an example:

"Draw a picture of a house with a chimney. Now add two more windows, three trees, and another chimney. Put a sidewalk in front."

9. Blobs

Ask students to think of a word and write three sentences using it. Then have them read their sentences aloud, substituting the word *blob* for the word. Have other students try to guess what the original word is. Here is an example:

The *blob* shone in the sky.
There was a full *blob* last night.
We danced by the light of the *blob*.

10. Scrambled Sentences

Write the words of a sentence in scrambled order. Have students race to unscramble them. Then, have them scramble their own sentences for each other to unscramble.

Name _____

Put an X on the line if the two words mean almost the same thing.

1. fat   wide   _____
2. rabbit   bunny   _____
3. sad   happy   _____
4. chair   seat   _____
5. tall   short   _____
6. fast   slow   _____
7. speedy   quick   _____
8. could   didn't   _____

9. might   may   _____
10. often   never   _____
11. feet   shoe   _____
12. strong   weak   _____
13. icy   cold   _____
14. smart   clever   _____
15. nice   ugly   _____
16. bus   dog   _____

17. cake   pig   _____
18. cow   calf   _____
19. cat   kitten   _____
20. rug   carpet   _____
21. new   used   _____
22. note   letter   _____
23. wood   saw   _____
24. fire   flame   _____

Main Idea Maneuvers, © 1986 David S. Lake Publishers

◯ = too easy   ☐ = too hard   △ = just right

7

Skill: Identifying repetition and redundancy

Name _____

Put an X on the line if the two words mean almost the same thing.

1. rock   stone   _____

2. shop   store   _____

3. boat   ship   _____

4. jump   swim   _____

5. sock   sack   _____

6. lot   little   _____

7. bag   sack   _____

8. sick   ill   _____

9. job   work   _____

10. cup   mug   _____

11. gift   present   _____

12. pants   slacks   _____

13. mile   inch   _____

14. walk   hike   _____

15. cook   bake   _____

16. shovel   dime   _____

17. smile   grin   _____

18. glue   paste   _____

19. throw   toss   _____

20. sea   ocean   _____

21. penny   coin   _____

22. bloom   blossom   _____

23. wash   clean   _____

24. cold   chilly   _____

8   ◯ = too easy   ▢ = too hard   △ = just right

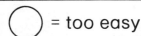

Skill: Identifying repetition and redundancy

Main Idea Maneuvers, © 1986 David S. Lake Publishers

Name _____

Put an X on the line if the two sentences mean almost the same thing.

1. My mom likes pizza.

   My mom enjoys pizza. _____

2. I am seven years old.

   I have had seven birthdays. _____

3. Jan is the best runner.

   The winner of the race is Jan. _____

4. The big dog took a nap.

   The large dog ate some meat. _____

5. The ground was wet after the rain.

   The rain made the ground damp. _____

6. This story is not true.

   I like this story. _____

7. What is in the box?

   I want the gift now. _____

8. There is cake left on the plate.

   Some cake is still on the plate. _____

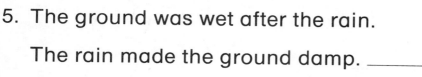

Main Idea Maneuvers, © 1986 David S. Lake Publishers

Skill: Identifying repetition and redundancy

Name _____

Put an X on the line if the two sentences mean almost the same thing.

1. I need a drink.

   I am thirsty. _____

2. Summer is very hot.

   It is hot in the summertime. _____

3. Tickets are not free.

   Tickets cost money. _____

4. Carla has a sore foot.

   Carla's foot is painful. _____

5. Push the door to go in.

   Open the door by pulling it. _____

6. I sleep in the upper bunk.

   My bunk is on top. _____

7. Look at the dog shake his tail!

   See that dog wag his tail! _____

8. The baby is getting sleepy.

   The baby is not drowsy. _____

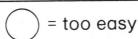 **10** ◯ = too easy   ▢ = too hard   △ = just right

Skill: Identifying repetition and redundancy

Main Idea Maneuvers, © 1986 David S. Lake Publishers

Name _____

Put an X by the word that means almost the same as the underlined word.

1. The boy was <u>weeping</u>.   cleaning _____   crying _____

2. Sue <u>liked</u> ice cream.   enjoyed _____   disliked _____

3. My hat is made of <u>cloth</u>.   wool _____   metal _____

4. You need a <u>sharp</u> pencil.   stale _____   pointed _____

5. Don't fall into the <u>pit</u>.   water _____   hole _____

6. I like to <u>wash</u> the table.   clean _____   set _____

7. Mike plays soccer <u>often</u>.   never _____   daily _____

8. Lisa walked on the <u>path</u> in the woods.   trail _____   grass _____

9. You <u>may</u> see Mickey Mouse.   will _____   might _____

10. Some clever boys <u>fixed</u> the bike.   repaired _____   painted _____

11. The grass is <u>damp</u> today.   wet _____   green _____

12. Our <u>plane</u> leaves at noon.   bus _____   jet _____

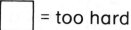
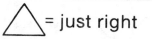

Skill: Identifying repetition and redundancy

Main Idea Maneuvers, © 1986 David S. Lake Publishers

Name _____

Next to each word, write another word
that has almost the same meaning.

1. happy _____

2. rabbit _____

3. quick _____

4. mother _____

5. warm _____

6. big _____

7. speedy _____

8. sleepy _____

9. cap _____ 16. sound _____

10. pond _____ 17. good _____

11. nap _____ 18. bad _____

12. breeze _____ 19. look _____

13. paste _____ 20. scream _____

14. say _____ 21. cord _____

15. road _____ 22. trash _____

12 ◯ = too easy ▢ = too hard △ = just right

Skill: Identifying repetition and redundancy

Main Idea Maneuvers, © 1986 David S. Lake Publishers

Name _____

1. Underline the words that tell **the dog was not small.**

    The big dog barked as Debbie walked by. He was so large that he looked like a wolf. Debbie thought the dog was the biggest animal she had ever seen.

2. Underline the words that tell **Bill went home fast.**

    Bill ran home from school. He wanted to play with his new ball. He hurried along. When Bill got home, he was tired because he had run all the way.

3. Underline the words that tell **I like to play.**

    I enjoy playing with small cars. I have fun with jump ropes, too. My best times are when my friends and I are playing.

4. Underline the words that tell **Ann was sick.**

    Ann did not feel well. She wanted to go to bed. Ann's head hurt and she felt sick. Her mother said she was ill.

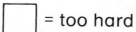

| ◯ = too easy | ▢ = too hard | △ = just right |

13

Main Idea Maneuvers, © 1986 David S. Lake Publishers

Skill: Identifying repetition and redundancy

1. Underline the words that tell **it was dark.**

    With only a few stars shining, the sky was dark. The sun was gone and there was no light. It was hard to see in the blackness.

2. Underline the words that tell **how Bruce feels about eating.**

    Bruce likes to eat. He enjoys lunch and looks forward to dinner. Snacks are nice for him, too.

3. Underline the words that tell **Celeste was not weak.**

    Celeste was very strong. She used her big muscles to carry things. Her friends said she was tough.

4. Underline the words that tell **my home and school are close.**

    My home is near the school. I live close to the playground. When I walk home from school, I do not walk far.

14

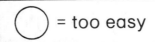 ⃝ = too easy   ▢ = too hard   △ = just right

Skill: Identifying repetition and redundancy

Main Idea Maneuvers, © 1986 David S. Lake Publishers

Name _____

Circle the word that does not fit.

1. nose   leg   eyes   ears

2. late   before   then   happy

3. over   near   under   what

4. tree   green   plant   bush

5. rock   stone   shell   pebble

6. rain   flood   water   thunder

7. beak   claw   feather   wind

8. sad   unhappy   mad   glad

◯ = too easy   ▢ = too hard   △ = just right

15

Skill: Determining relevance

Name _____

Circle the word that does not fit.

1. bed   book   table   chair

2. dog   cat   horse   state

3. mine   his   yours   play

4. run   jump   rope   hop

5. cup   cow   plate   dish

6. swim   paint   draw   color

7. bee   honey   fly   wasp

8. flat   smooth   bumpy   red

16

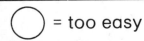 = too easy	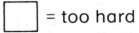 = too hard	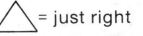 = just right

Skill: Determining relevance

Main Idea Maneuvers, © 1986 David S. Lake Publishers

Name _____

Draw a different picture in each box to
show what the word means.

1. pets

2. home

3. school

4. fast

17

Main Idea Maneuvers, © 1986 David S. Lake Publishers

Skill: Determining relevance

Name _____

Draw a different picture in each box to show what the word means.

1. zoo

2. food

3. toys

4. people

18

Main Idea Maneuvers, © 1986 David S. Lake Publishers

◯ = too easy   ☐ = too hard   △ = just right

Skill: Determining relevance

Name _____

Write two words that belong in each group.

1. things you can eat   _____   _____

2. things you can wear   _____   _____

3. things that have wings   _____   _____

4. things that are red   _____   _____

5. foods that are sweet   _____   _____

6. things that are wet   _____   _____

7. toys that have wheels   _____   _____

8. kinds of pets   _____   _____

9. kinds of jobs   _____   _____

10. things in the sky   _____   _____

11. things used for play   _____   _____

12. places to work   _____   _____

Main Idea Maneuvers, © 1986 David S. Lake Publishers

◯ = too easy   ▢ = too hard   △ = just right

19

Skill: Determining relevance

Name _____

Underline the words that tell **how.**

1. The man left in a hurry.

2. Pat shook her head sadly.

3. Slowly, the flag went up.

4. Joe smiled happily when he won.

5. The camper stood bravely near the bear.

6. Suddenly, the lights went out.

7. Luckily, we found a place to buy gas.

8. Kelly talked loudly in the library.

20

| ◯ = too easy | ▢ = too hard | △ = just right |

Skill: Determining relevance

Name 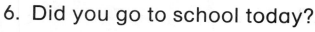 _____

Underline the words that tell **when.**

1. We worked hard all day.

2. The man will run faster next time.

3. In a few days, we will play ball.

4. Last summer, I went to the beach.

5. You may wash your hands before you eat.

6. Did you go to school today?

7. My mother works hard every day.

8. We see many flowers in May.

21

Main Idea Maneuvers, © 1986 David S. Lake Publishers

Skill: Determining relevance

Name _____

Underline the words that tell **where.**

1. We went into the water to cool off.

2. The bird sang near the top of the tree.

3. Put the paper under the book.

4. Over the table was a fine cloth.

5. We ate lunch at the old rest stop.

6. How does Don drive down the road?

7. A large rock is in your path.

8. Feed the animals beside the cage.

22 ⬭ = too easy ▢ = too hard △ = just right

Skill: Determining relevance

Main Idea Maneuvers, © 1986 David S. Lake Publishers

Name _____

Underline the words that tell **who.**

1. The first people came to school early.

2. Are those toys for Andy and me?

3. Ben Franklin was born in 1706.

4. The books were read by first-graders.

5. Lucy wanted to go home.

6. Let everybody play on the swings.

7. They left the party early.

8. My older sister likes to travel.

Who is this?

○ = too easy   ☐ = too hard   △ = just right

23

Main Idea Maneuvers, © 1986 David S. Lake Publishers

Skill: Determining relevance

Name _____

Draw a different picture in each box to show what the words mean.

1. things in the sky

2. things you can ride

3. things used for cooking

4. people who work

24

○ = too easy   □ = too hard   △ = just right

Skill: Classifying nouns

Main Idea Maneuvers, © 1986 David S. Lake Publishers

Name _____

Draw a different picture in each box to show what the words mean.

1. kinds of clothing

2. types of shoes

3. things that make music

4. tools for building

◯ = too easy   ▢ = too hard   △ = just right

25

Skill: Classifying nouns

Name _____

Tell how the words belong together.

1. wagon
   truck
   bus   _____

2. racket
   ball
   net   _____

3. hammer
   saw
   nail   _____

4. flashlight
   lantern
   lamp   _____

5. cat
   bird
   dog   _____

6. spoon
   plate
   bowl   _____

7. cookies
   candy
   cake   _____

8. brush
   hairpin
   comb   _____

26

 = too easy   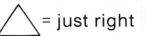 = too hard   △ = just right

Skill: Classifying nouns

Main Idea Maneuvers © 1986 David S. Lake Publishers

Name _____

Tell how the words belong together.

1. raincoat
   umbrella
   boots _____

2. banana
   orange
   apple _____

3. sleeping bag
   tent
   cot _____

4. cheese
   ice cream
   milk _____

5. crayon
   chalk
   pen _____

6. window
   door
   roof _____

7. shampoo
   toothpaste
   soap _____

8. Mary
   Susan
   Sara _____

Main Idea Maneuvers, © 1986 David S. Lake Publishers

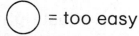 = too easy   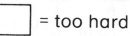 = too hard   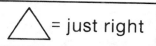 = just right

27

Skill: Classifying nouns

Name _____

List three things that show what the
word or words mean.

1. names of boys

   _____

   _____

   _____

2. colors

   _____

   _____

   _____

3. things to read

   _____

   _____

   _____

4. animals

   _____

   _____

5. picnic things

   _____

   _____

   _____

6. tools

   _____

   _____

   _____

7. things found in the water

   _____

   _____

   _____

8. flowers

   _____

   _____

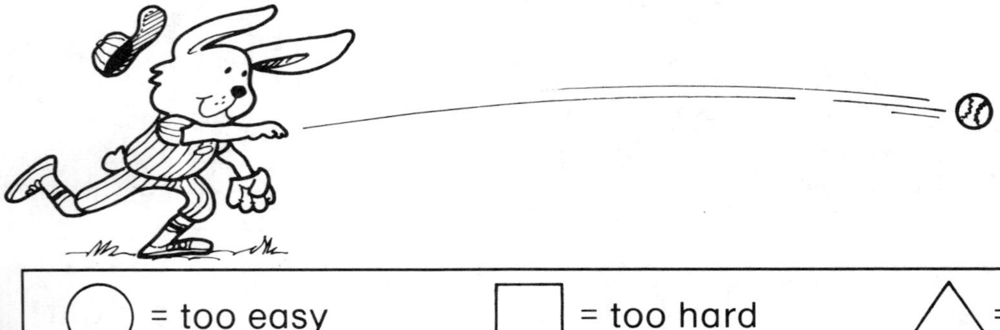

28

◯ = too easy	▢ = too hard	△ = just right

Skill: Classifying nouns

Name _____

List three things that show what the
word or words mean.

1. fruit

_____

_____

_____

2. items used for carrying

_____

_____

_____

3. food for breakfast

_____

_____

_____

4. items in the hospital

_____

_____

_____

5. baby things

_____

_____

_____

6. things used for cleaning

_____

_____

_____

7. things on the playground

_____

_____

_____

8. things that are not safe

_____

_____

_____

◯ = too easy   ☐ = too hard   △ = just right

29

Skill: Classifying nouns

Name _____

For each sentence, underline the words that form a list. Tell how the words belong together.

1. A doctor, a nurse, and a dentist rushed in.

   _____

2. My father needs a mop, a sponge, and a cloth now.

   _____

3. Let's take Paul, Sid, and Tom to the movies.

   _____

4. We saw hats, horns, and a cake at the party.

   _____

5. The zoo was full of lions, bears, and monkeys.

   _____

30

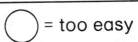 = too easy   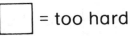 = too hard   △ = just right

Skill: Classifying nouns

Main Idea Maneuvers, © 1986 David S. Lake Publishers

Name _____

For each sentence, underline the words that form a list. Tell how the words belong together.

1. In the morning we eat bread, fruit, and cereal.

   _____

2. You need to bring a coat, a hat, and boots.

   _____

3. Betty, Joan, and Marie went home.

   _____

4. Chris used forks, spoons, and knives.

   _____

5. When will the letters, cards, and papers come?

   _____

◯ = too easy	▢ = too hard	△ = just right

31

Main Idea Maneuvers, © 1986 David S. Lake Publishers

Skill: Classifying nouns

Name _____

Draw a different picture in each box to show what the words mean.

1. playing in the snow

2. getting clean

3. camping in the woods

4. getting ready for school

32

○ = too easy ☐ = too hard △ = just right

Skill: Classifying series of events

Main Idea Maneuvers, © 1986 David S. Lake Publishers

Name _____

Draw a different picture in each box to
show what the words mean.

1. fixing
   your hair

2. giving
   a present

3. finding
   a coin

4. winning
   a race

◯ = too easy   ▢ = too hard   △ = just right

33

Main Idea Maneuvers, © 1986 David S. Lake Publishers

Skill: Classifying series of events

Name _____

Tell what is happening.

1. kicking
   hopping
   stamping

   _____

   _____

2. baking
   roasting
   frying

   _____

   _____

3. cutting
   pasting
   coloring

   _____

   _____

4. counting
   adding
   subtracting

   _____

   _____

5. napping
   snoring
   dreaming

   _____

   _____

34

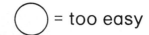 = too easy    = too hard   △ = just right

Skill: Classifying series of events

Main Idea Maneuvers, © 1986 David S. Lake Publishers

Name _____

Tell what is happening.

1. running
   falling
   crying

   _____
   _____

2. hammering
   sawing
   measuring

   _____
   _____

3. yelling
   singing
   talking

   _____
   _____

4. waving
   clapping
   pointing

   _____
   _____

5. biting
   chewing
   swallowing

   _____
   _____

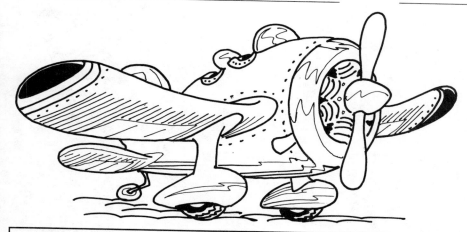

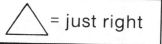

◯ = too easy   ☐ = too hard   △ = just right

35

Skill: Classifying series of events

Name _____

List three steps for each activity below.

1. flying a kite

_____

_____

2. digging a hole

_____

_____

3. taking a picture

_____

_____

4. eating lunch

_____

_____

5. having a party

_____

_____

_____

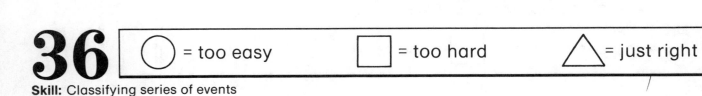

36

◯ = too easy   ☐ = too hard   △ = just right

Skill: Classifying series of events

Main Idea Maneuvers, © 1986 David S. Lake Publishers

Name _____

List three steps for each activity below.

1. taking a trip

   _____

   _____

   _____

2. making cookies

   _____

   _____

   _____

3. going to school

   _____

   _____

   _____

4. going swimming

   _____

   _____

   _____

5. building a house

   _____

   _____

   _____

◯ = too easy   ▢ = too hard   △ = just right

37

Skill: Classifying series of events

Name _____

Underline the series of events. Tell what the sentence is about.

1. The baby stood up, took a step, and fell down.

   _____

2. Joe got bread, opened a jar of jelly, and used a knife.

   _____

3. Our team had the ball, ran fast, and won the game.

   _____

4. The dog sat up, barked, and took the treat.

   _____

5. Sandy opened the lunch box, unwrapped the sandwich, and took a bite.

   _____

38

| ◯ = too easy | ☐ = too hard | △ = just right |

Skill: Classifying series of events

Main Idea Maneuvers, © 1986 David S. Lake Publishers

Name _____

Underline the series of events. Tell what
the sentence is about.

1. The gun went off, the boys ran, and the fans
   cheered.

   _____

2. Rain came down, the streets flooded, and
   things were washed away.

   _____

3. The fire fighters came quickly, used big
   hoses, and put the fire out.

   _____

4. I opened the book, read slowly, and looked at the pictures.

5. We gave the woman money, took our bag, and left the store.

   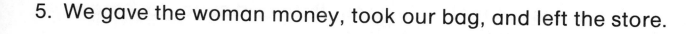

Main Idea Maneuvers, © 1986 David S. Lake Publishers

◯ = too easy   ▢ = too hard   △ = just right

39

Skill: Classifying series of events

Name _____

Copy the sentence that tells what each
passage is about.

1. Try to be nice to other people. Help them when you can. Don't
   say mean things.

   _____

   _____

2. We like to eat fish. We also like cake. We like many kinds of food.

   _____

   _____

3. Last night the sky was dark. There was a scary sound. I was
   afraid last night!

   _____

   _____

4. Cookies are easy to make. First, put flour and sugar together.
   Add butter. Then, bake the cookies.

   _____

   _____

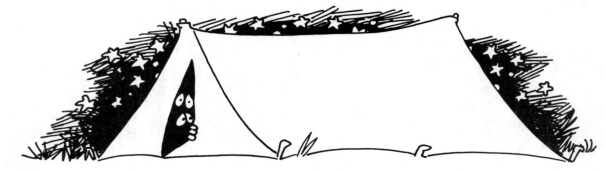

40 | 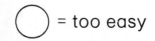 = too easy | ☐ = too hard | △ = just right |

Main Idea Maneuvers, © 1986 David S. Lake Publishers

Skill: Identifying topic sentences

Name _____

Copy the sentence that tells what each passage is about.

1. I play with my cat. First, I throw a small ball. My cat runs after it. Then, I pull the ball away from the cat's claws.

   _____

   _____

2. Some people are very strong. They can lift heavy things. Their muscles are big. These people can move heavy objects.

   _____

   _____

3. The flowers looked nice. We picked them and put them in a vase. We had red ones and yellow ones.

   _____

   _____

4. Jenny opened the candy jar carefully. She took one piece out. She chewed slowly. Jenny enjoyed the candy.

   _____

   _____

Main Idea Maneuvers, © 1986 David S. Lake Publishers

◯ = too easy   ☐ = too hard   △ = just right

41

Name _____

Copy the sentence that tells what each
passage is about.

1. Newspapers tell about the world. They tell about what happens
   each day. Newspapers also tell what will happen soon.

   _____

   _____

2. My brother made lunch today. He smiled when he gave me some
   soup and a sandwich. He made the same things for himself.

   _____

   _____

3. Henry's bird died. The bird was old and sick. Henry loved his
   bird. He cried when it died.

   _____

   _____

4. I like to swim. You like to play in the sand. We like to walk by the
   water. We enjoy the beach!

   _____

   _____

42 ◯ = too easy ☐ = too hard △ = just right

Skill: Identifying topic sentences

Main Idea Maneuvers, © 1986 David S. Lake Publishers

Copy the sentence that tells what each
passage is about.

1. My new dress is too short. It is hard to put on. It looks funny. My
   new dress does not fit.

   _____

   _____

2. My friend works hard. She drives a tractor. She takes care of
   animals. She plants a big garden.

   _____

   _____

3. Buy a zinky toy! You will have fun with it. Lots of boys and girls
   have one. Zinky toys do not cost much.

   _____

   _____

4. The last time I drank a soda was in the summer. It was a hot day.
   I hoped the soda would cool me off.

   _____

   _____

◯ = too easy   ▢ = too hard   △ = just right

43

Skill: Identifying topic sentences

Name _____

Draw a picture in each box. Under each box write one sentence to tell about your picture.

1. _____

_____

2. _____

_____

44

◯ = too easy   ▢ = too hard   △ = just right

Skill: Inventing topic sentences

Main Idea Maneuvers, © 1986 David S. Lake Publishers

Name _____

For each group of words, write a sentence to tell how the words belong together.

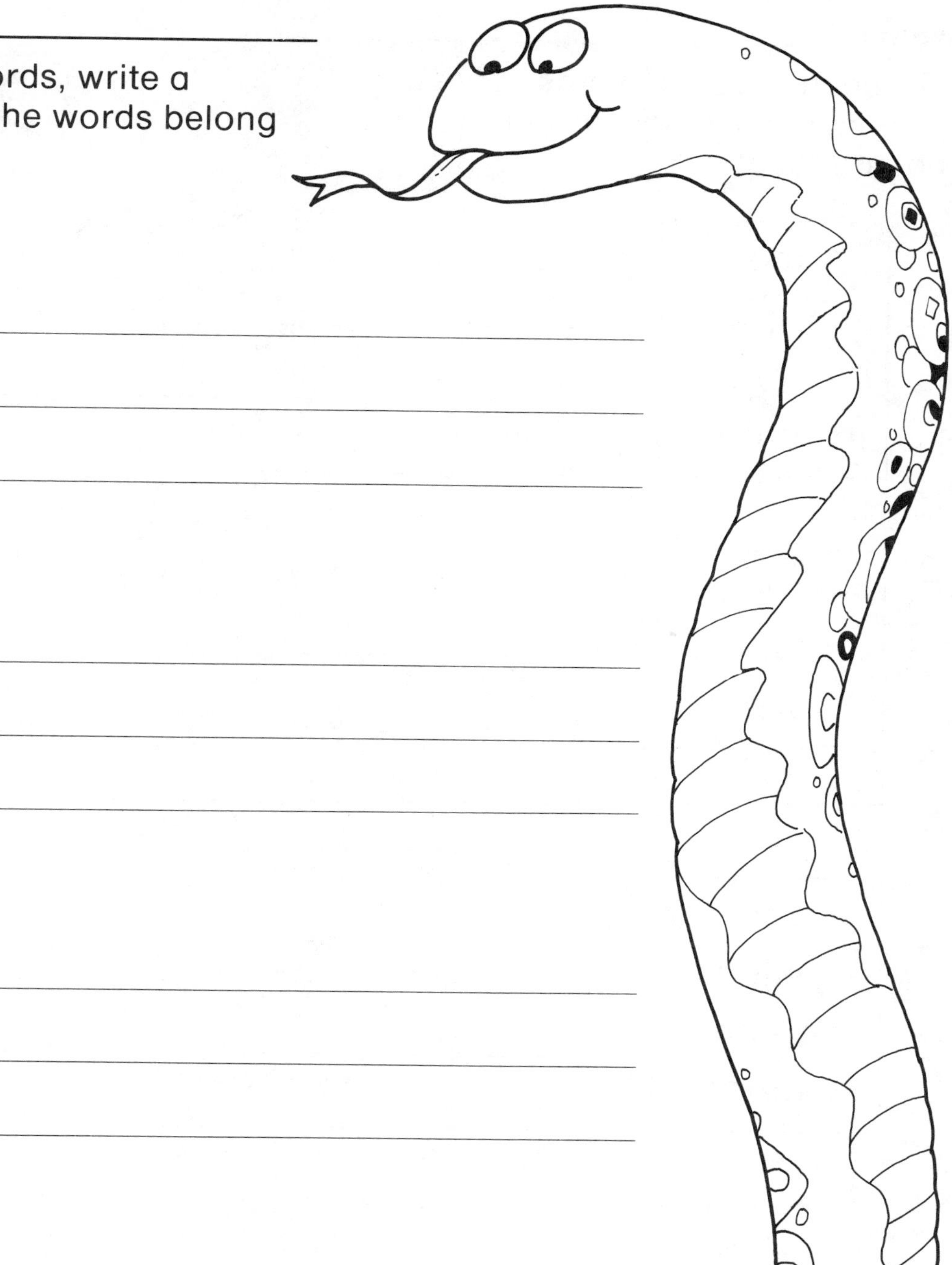

1. | hat
coat
pants
shoes |

_____
_____
_____

2. | happy
glad
smile
enjoy |

_____
_____
_____

3. | fire
burn
hot
heat |

_____
_____
_____

4. | late
last
behind
end |

_____
_____
_____

◯ = too easy   ▢ = too hard   △ = just right

45

Skill: Inventing topic sentences

Name _____

For each group of words, write a
sentence to tell how the words
belong together.

1.
| ice |
| snow |
| frost |
| ice cream |

_____
_____
_____

2.
| run |
| jump |
| play |
| swing |

_____
_____
_____

3.
| red |
| yellow |
| green |
| blue |

_____
_____
_____

4.
| throw |
| hit |
| ball |
| mitt |

_____
_____
_____

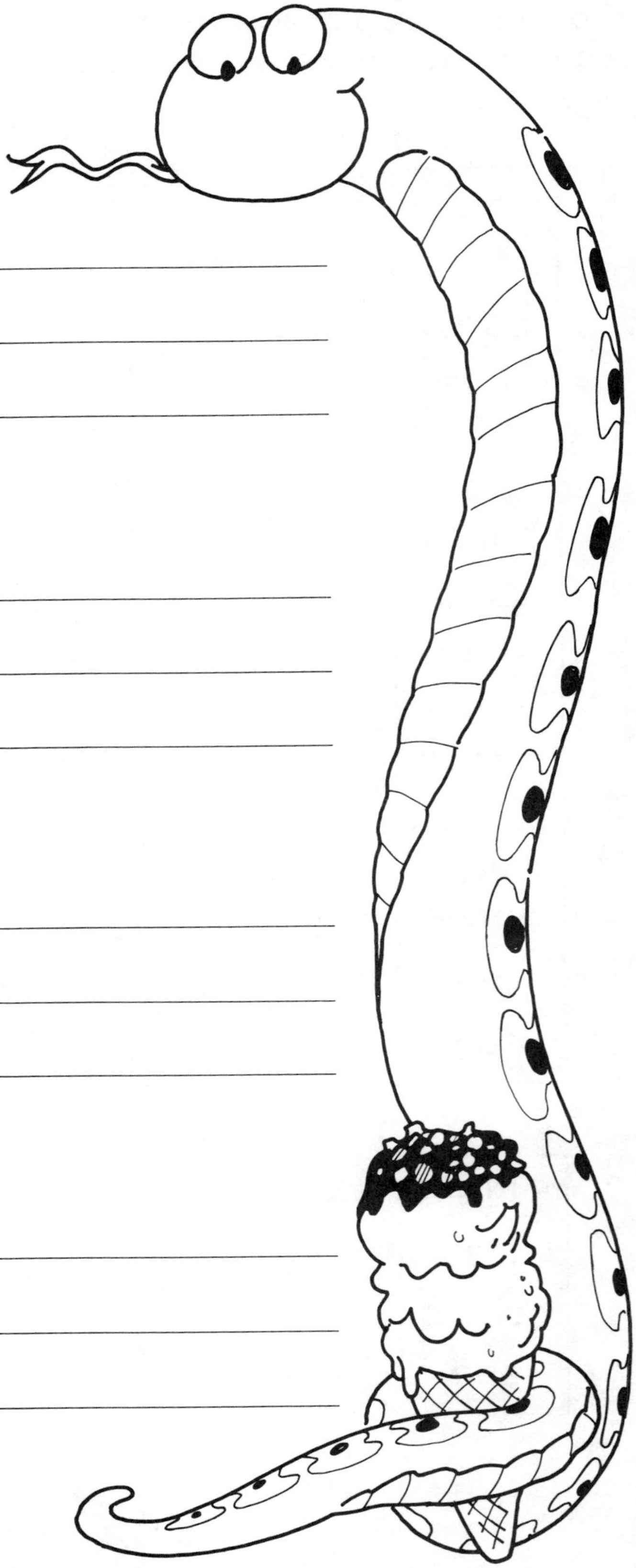

46

○ = too easy   □ = too hard   △ = just right

Skill: Inventing topic sentences

Main Idea Maneuvers, © 1986 David S. Lake Publishers

...cked a bag. He put in socks, pants, shirts,
...he toothbrush. Jim took the bag with him
...he left the house.

_____

_____

2. The baby was crying. Dad gave the baby some food. Then he held her close for a while. The baby went to sleep.

_____

_____

3. Boys and girls came out of the classroom. They ran to the playground. Some children went over to the swings.

_____

_____

4. That is a pretty box. Is it a gift? Is it something that is alive? I want to know what is in that box.

_____

_____

◯ = too easy   ▢ = too hard   △ = just right

47

Skill: Inventing topic sentences

Name _____

Underline the answer that best tells
about each group of words.

1.
rabbit
fox
squirrel

a. animal pets
b. animals in the woods
c. my pets

2.
can
box
bag

a. things used for cooking
b. things to hold other things
c. toys for children

3.
wagon
ball
bike

a. toys with wheels
b. toys for babies
c. outside toys

4.
banana
orange
apple

a. food for lunch
b. fruit
c. food I like

5.
blanket
pillow
sheet

a. warm things
b. things to take on a trip
c. bed things

48

○ = too easy   □ = too hard   △ = just right

Skill: Identifying main idea

Main Idea Maneuvers, © 1986 David S. Lake Publishers

Name _____

Underline the answer that best tells about each group of words.

1.
| gallop |
| trot |
| run |

  a. things that make music
  b. ways a horse moves
  c. kinds of dancing

2.
| beside |
| near |
| close |

  a. under
  b. over
  c. nearby

3.
| bad |
| evil |
| wicked |

  a. kind
  b. nice
  c. not good

4.
| rushed |
| ran |
| hurried |

  a. went quickly
  b. wanted to play
  c. went home

5.
| napping |
| dozing |
| sleeping |

  a. being quiet
  b. moving slowly
  c. taking a rest

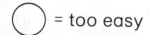 = too easy   ☐ = too hard   △ = just right

49

Skill: Identifying main idea

Name _____

Underline the answer that best tells about each group of words.

1.
| elephant |
| tiger |
| monkey |

a. wild animals
b. pets
c. animals that fly

2.
| jelly |
| jam |
| honey |

a. food we like
b. food with salt
c. food that is sweet

3.
| cry |
| frown |
| weep |

a. being glad
b. being silly
c. being sad

4.
| said |
| asked |
| told |

a. Someone spoke.
b. He was told.
c. We want to know.

5.
| dig |
| plow |
| hoe |

a. working inside
b. working in dirt
c. playing at school

50

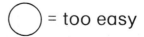 = too easy    = too hard   △ = just right

Skill: Identifying main idea

Main Idea Maneuvers, © 1986 David S. Lake Publishers

Name _____

Underline the answer that best tells
about each group of words.

1.
green
red
purple

   a. names of colors
b. paints
c. crayons

2.
paper
pencil
eraser

   a. a nice present
b. writing things
c. coloring things

3.
she
her
Miss

   a. words about my friend
b. short words
c. words about a woman

4.
first
next
later

   a. words that tell when
b. words that tell who
c. spelling words

5.
smiling
happy
glad

   a. not pretty
b. not sad
c. not good

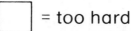

○ = too easy   □ = too hard   △ = just right

51

Main Idea Maneuvers, © 1986 David S. Lake Publishers

Skill: Identifying main idea

Name _____

Draw a picture to show each idea. Put at least four things in each picture.

1. having a party

2. going swimming

3. taking care of animals

○ = too easy   ☐ = too hard   △ = just right

Skill: Identifying main idea

Main Idea Maneuvers, © 1986 David S. Lake Publishers

Name _____

Draw a picture to show each idea. Put at least four things in each picture.

1. helping at home

2. traveling

3. being happy

◯ = too easy   ▢ = too hard   △ = just right

53

Skill: Identifying main idea

Name _____

Draw a picture to show each idea. Put at least four things in each picture.

1. a circus

2. something
   scary

3. my best friend

54

○ = too easy □ = too hard △ = just right

Skill: Identifying main idea

Name _____

Make up a title for each of these things.

1. your best place to play

_____

_____

2. a refrigerator

_____

_____

3. a book about you

_____

_____

4. a story about your school

_____

5. a magazine for children

_____

6. your best toy

_____

◯ = too easy	▢ = too hard	△ = just right

55

Skill: Understanding and using titles

Name _____

Make up a title for each of these things.

1. a cookbook for food to go in lunch boxes

   _____

   _____

2. a special day at the zoo

   _____

   _____

3. a television show

   _____

   _____

4. a breakfast food

   _____

5. a book about living on the moon

   _____

6. a scary story

   _____

56 $\bigcirc$ = too easy $\square$ = too hard $\triangle$ = just right

Skill: Understanding and using titles

Main Idea Maneuvers, © 1986 David S. Lake Publishers

Name _____

Write three sentences about each book.

Best Friends

1. _____
   _____
   _____
   _____
   _____
   _____

Ouch!

2. _____
   _____
   _____
   _____
   _____
   _____

Do Not Touch

3. _____
   _____
   _____
   _____
   _____
   _____

◯ = too easy   ▢ = too hard   △ = just right

57

Skill: Understanding and using titles

Name _____

Write three sentences about each book.

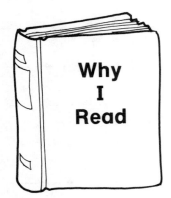

**Why
I
Read**

1. _____
_____
_____
_____
_____
_____
_____

**All
About
Me**

2. _____
_____
_____
_____
_____
_____
_____

Jokes

3. _____
_____
_____
_____
_____
_____
_____

58 ⬜ ◯ = too easy ⬜ = too hard △ = just right

Main Idea Maneuvers, © 1986 David S. Lake Publishers

Skill: Understanding and using titles

Answer Key

Page 7
The following pairs of words should have an X on the line:
1, 2, 4, 7, 9, 13, 14, 18, 19, 20, 22, and 24.

Page 8
The following pairs of words should have an X on the line:
1, 2, 3, 7, 8, 9, 10, 11, 12, 14, 15, 17, 18, 19, 20, 21, 22, 23, and 24.

Page 9
The following pairs of sentences should have an X on the line:
1, 2, 3, 5, and 8.

Page 10
The following pairs of sentences should have an X on the line:
1, 2, 3, 4, 6, and 7.

Page 11
The following words should have an X on the line:
1. crying, 2. enjoyed, 3. wool, 4. pointed, 5. hole, 6. clean, 7. daily, 8. trail, 9. might, 10. repaired, 11. wet, 12. jet.

Page 12
Accept a synonym for each word.

Page 13
The following words should be underlined (accept some variation):
1. big, large, wolf, biggest; 2. ran, hurried, had run; 3. enjoy playing, have fun, best times; 4. did not feel well, wanted to go to bed, head hurt, felt sick, was ill.

Page 14
The following words should be underlined (accept some variation):
1. sky was dark, sun was gone, no light, hard to see, blackness; 2. likes to eat, enjoys lunch, looks forward to dinner, Snacks are nice; 3. very strong, big muscles, tough; 4. near, close, do not walk far.

Page 15
The following words should be circled:
1. leg, 2. happy, 3. what, 4. green, 5. shell, 6. thunder, 7. wind, 8. glad.

Page 16

The following words should be circled:
1. book, 2. state, 3. play, 4. rope, 5. cow,
6. swim, 7. honey, 8. red.

Page 17

Accept appropriate pictures.

Page 18

Accept appropriate pictures.

Page 19

Accept appropriate nouns.

Page 20

The following words should be underlined:
1. in a hurry, 2. sadly, 3. Slowly,
4. happily, 5. bravely, 6. Suddenly,
7. Luckily, 8. loudly.

Page 21

The following words should be underlined:
1. all day, 2. next time, 3. In a few days,
4. Last summer, 5. before you eat,
6. today, 7. every day, 8. in May.

Page 22

The following words should be underlined:
1. into the water, 2. near the top of the tree, 3. under the book, 4. Over the table,
5. at the old rest stop, 6. down the road,
7. in your path, 8. beside the cage.

Page 23

The following words should be underlined:
1. The first people, 2. Andy and me,
3. Ben Franklin, 4. first-graders, 5. Lucy,
6. everybody, 7. They, 8. My older sister.

Page 24

Accept appropriate pictures.

Page 25

Accept appropriate pictures.

Page 26

Accept variations of the following answers:
1. things with wheels, 2. things used in tennis, 3. tools, 4. lights, 5. pets, 6. things used for eating, 7. sweet foods, 8. things used for hair.

Page 27

Accept variations of the following answers:
1. things used in the rain, 2. fruit,
3. things used for camping, 4. dairy foods, 5. writing tools, 6. parts of a building, 7. cleansers, 8. girls' names.

Page 28

Accept appropriate nouns.

Page 29

Accept appropriate nouns.

Page 30

The following words should be underlined and explained (accept some variation in the wording of how the words belong together):
1. doctor, nurse, dentist (people involved with medicine); 2. mop, sponge, cloth (cleaning supplies); 3. Paul, Sid, Tom (boys' names); 4. hats, horns, cake (party things); 5. lions, bears, monkeys (animals).

Page 31

The following words should be underlined and explained (accept some variation in the wording of how the words belong together):
1. bread, fruit, cereal (breakfast foods);
2. coat, hat, boots (clothing); 3. Betty, Joan, Marie (girls' names); 4. forks, spoons, knives (tools for meals); 5. letters, cards, papers (mail).

Page 32

Accept appropriate pictures.

Page 33

Accept appropriate pictures.

Page 34

Accept some variation of the following answers:
1. moving feet, 2. cooking, 3. working on a project (as art), 4. working in arithmetic, 5. sleeping.

Page 35

Accept some variation of the following answers:
1. falling down, 2. building something, 3. making sounds, 4. moving hands, 5. eating.

Page 36

Accept appropriate answers.

Page 37

Accept appropriate answers.

Page 38

The following words should be underlined and explained (accept some variation in the wording of what the events are about):
1. stood up, took a step, fell down (learning to walk); 2. got bread, opened a jar of jelly, used a knife (making a snack); 3. had the ball, ran fast, won the game (playing a game); 4. sat up, barked, took the treat (doing a trick); 5. opened the lunch box, unwrapped the sandwich, took a bite (starting lunch).

Page 39

The following words should be underlined and explained (accept some variation in the wording of what the events are about):
1. gun went off, boys ran, fans cheered (a race); 2. Rain came down, streets flooded, things were washed away (a rainstorm); 3. fire fighters came quickly, used big hoses, put the fire out (putting out a fire); 4. opened the book, read slowly, looked at the pictures (reading a book); 5. gave the woman money, took our bag, left the store (shopping).

Page 40

1. Try to be nice to other people.
2. We like many kinds of food.
3. I was afraid last night!
4. Cookies are easy to make.

Page 41

1. I play with my cat.
2. Some people are very strong.
3. The flowers looked nice.
4. Jenny enjoyed the candy.

Page 42

1. Newspapers tell about the world.
2. My brother made lunch today.
3. Henry's bird died.
4. We enjoy the beach!

Page 43

1. My new dress does not fit.
2. My friend works hard.
3. Buy a zinky toy!
4. The last time I drank a soda was in the summer.

Page 44

Accept appropriate pictures and answers.

Page 45

Accept appropriate answers.

Page 46

Accept appropriate answers.

Page 47

Accept appropriate answers.

Page 48

The following answers should be underlined:
1. b, 2. b, 3. c, 4. b, 5. c.

Page 49
The following answers should be underlined:
1. b, 2. c, 3. c, 4. a, 5. c.

Page 50
The following answers should be underlined:
1. a, 2. c, 3. c, 4. a, 5. b.

Page 51
The following answers should be underlined:
1. a, 2. b, 3. c, 4. a, 5. b.

Page 52
Accept appropriate pictures.

Page 53
Accept appropriate pictures.

Page 54
Accept appropriate pictures.

Page 55
Accept appropriate answers.

Page 56
Accept appropriate answers.

Page 57
Accept appropriate answers.

Page 58
Accept appropriate answers.

Main Idea Maneuvers © 1986 David S. Lake Publishers

Making Tracks to Main Idea

Grades 4–6

Contents

Introduction

The lessons in this workbook develop eight subskills for determining main idea. The worksheets are organized by section, each section focusing on one of the eight subskills.

1. **Identifying Repetition and Redundancy**
2. **Determining Relevance**
3. **Classifying Nouns**
4. **Classifying Series of Events**
5. **Identifying Topic Sentences**
6. **Inventing Topic Sentences**
7. **Identifying Main Idea**
8. **Understanding and Using Titles**

At the conclusion of each activity is an evaluation code box.

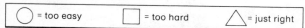

An evaluation of item difficulty can be made by enclosing the item number within one of the shapes shown in the box to relay the coded message. Another way to use the code box is simply to shade in the shape that best evaluates the page. This evaluation might be made by the teacher, the student, a tutor, or a team. The code is designed to help determine skill areas needing further attention.

The following section suggests additional activities for continued practice in the subskills necessary for identifying main ideas and in understanding and using titles.

Additional Activities

1. Semantic Mapping
Have students make a diagram with a superordinate word in the center circle, as indicated below. Then have them fill in the rest of the diagram. This activity is useful for prereading, reading, and postreading.

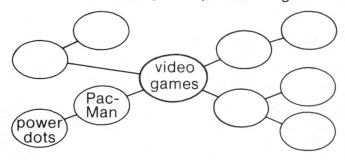

2. Sentence Development
Have students write sentences according to a pattern. Here is an example:

who + did what + how + where + when

Felicia watched a movie happily at home last night.

3. Naming and Listing
Have students make lists, verbal or written, on topics such as the following:

items that are sharp
names of fish
towns in your state
things that are red

4. Reminiscences
Have the students tell about past experiences, using such topics as the following:
My Worst Punishment
My First Bus Ride
My Best Birthday
My Hobby

5. Sequential Stories
Have one student write the first sentence of a story. Then have other students add one sentence each. Finally, read the story aloud and discuss how stories can be written.

6. Emotional Words
Have students read a passage and ask them to describe their own emotions as they read. Then have them answer the following questions:

Would you want to live next door to the main character?

Why do you think as you do?

How does the author feel about an event or character?

How do you know?

Have students look for words that indicate feelings and either list or underline them.

7. Menus
Have students write a menu with a specific purpose. Here are some examples:

lunch for vegetarians
dinner at a dairy-food restaurant
a picnic for four people

8. Name the Ways
Ask students a question that requires a list of words as an answer. Divide class into teams and have each team try to come up with the greatest number of possibilities. Here are some examples:

In what ways can a horse move? (gallop, trot, walk, canter, prance, and so on)

How does wood feel? (smooth, splintery, wet, dry, rough, bumpy, and so on)

9. Thank You!
Have students group adjectives under the headings "Thank you!" and "No, thank you!" according to whether or not the adjectives are complimentary. Here are some examples:

Thank you!	*No, thank you!*
friendly	silly
helpful	selfish
hardworking	pushy

10. Picture Vocabulary
Draw the outline of a figure, name it, and then have students fill it with descriptive words. Here are some examples:

My Teacher

My House

Name _____

Circle the word that means almost the same as the word in dark type. Use a dictionary if you need help.

1. **like**   enjoy   discover
2. **big**   scary   huge
3. **give**   award   take
4. **feast**   banquet   birthday
5. **beach**   water   shore
6. **belief**   faith   desire
7. **bend**   curve   straighten
8. **break**   burst   carry
9. **error**   mistake   patch
10. **people**   persons   workers
11. **pinch**   squeeze   collect
12. **stout**   stupid   sturdy
13. **youthful**   young   less
14. **zenith**   summit   big
15. **refuse**   reject   accept
16. **flimsy**   silky   weak
17. **flood**   deluge   trouble
18. **enough**   plenty   equal
19. **device**   invention   problem
20. **consult**   confer   congregate

21. **control**   restrain   punish
22. **complete**   thorough   complex
23. **answer**   achieve   reply
24. **anger**   wrath   escape
25. **alter**   change   marry
26. **fond**   loving   magnificent
27. **fluid**   liquid   solid
28. **program**   present   schedule
29. **holy**   sacred   empty
30. **rustic**   rural   restful
31. **rich**   wealthy   nice
32. **common**   usual   interesting
33. **unite**   join   fix
34. **ancient**   old   secret
35. **clumsy**   awkward   graceful
36. **conceal**   hide   destroy

⭕ = too easy   ▭ = too hard   △ = just right

7

Making Tracks to Main Idea, © 1986 David S. Lake Publishers

Skill: Identifying repetition and redundancy

Name _____

Circle the word that means almost the same as the word in dark type. Use a dictionary if you need help.

1. **follow**	pursue	desire					
2. **lead**	guide	cooperate					
3. **reject**	repeat	refuse					
4. **defeat**	destroy	deliver					
5. **transfer**	change	mix		21. **battle**	fight	soldier
6. **shy**	timid	bold		22. **balance**	weigh	quay
7. **topic**	idol	theme		23. **forget**	overlook	employ
8. **chuckle**	laugh	agree		24. **foreign**	strange	similar
9. **clever**	clear	skillful		25. **finish**	complete	waver
10. **dismal**	gloomy	elated		26. **invalid**	healthy	sickly
11. **cheat**	deceive	joke		27. **locate**	find	change
12. **brag**	boost	boast		28. **lower**	decrease	climb
13. **deliver**	transmit	receive		29. **lie**	falsehood	escape
14. **familiar**	known	likable		30. **insane**	crazy	reliable
15. **fact**	truth	guess		31. **loud**	noisy	timid
16. **quiet**	calm	quick		32. **mainly**	mostly	pointed
17. **raise**	elevate	pay		33. **mask**	cover	clown
18. **religion**	faith	area		34. **middle**	midst	end
19. **praise**	commend	complain		35. **power**	pirate	force
20. **terrible**	horrible	interesting		36. **prize**	award	report

8   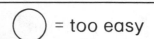 = too easy   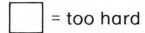 = too hard   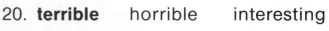 = just right

Skill: Identifying repetition and redundancy

Making Tracks to Main Idea, © 1986 David S. Lake Publishers

Name _____

Write a word that means almost the same as
the underlined word. Use a dictionary if you need help.

1. Please <u>fetch</u> another basket of apples. _____

2. The man's <u>business</u> was selling computers. _____

3. These students are <u>brilliant</u> in math. _____

4. We need an <u>ally</u> in our time of trouble. _____

5. Sarah <u>mourned</u> when her pet died. _____

6. There was a strange <u>peace</u> after the storm. _____

7. Mike understood the lesson <u>perfectly</u>. _____

8. The doctor discovered a new <u>remedy</u>. _____

9. It is time to say <u>farewell</u>. _____

10. The <u>vacant</u> lot is a great place to play. _____

11. You may give a <u>donation</u> to charity. _____

12. We spun around until we were <u>giddy</u>. _____

Making Tracks to Main Idea, © 1986 David S. Lake Publishers

| ⭕ = too easy | ⬜ = too hard | △ = just right | **9** |

Skill: Identifying repetition and redundancy

Name _____

Write a word that means almost the same as
the underlined word. Use a dictionary if you need help.

1. Football is an outdoor <u>sport</u>.   _____

2. The disappearance was certainly <u>odd</u>.   _____

3. Let's try to <u>invent</u> a new machine.   _____

4. This <u>concert</u> will be open to the public.   _____

5. A good long trip will <u>renew</u> your spirits.   _____

6. Jennifer is no <u>relation</u> to me.   _____

7. We wanted to use the <u>single</u> remaining tool.   _____

8. Jason entered the <u>argument</u> just for spite.   _____

9. This instrument makes an interesting <u>sound</u>.   _____

10. Old fish can have a <u>powerful</u> smell.   _____

11. Let's <u>unite</u> our teams for this game.   _____

12. It is <u>uncommon</u> for Jack to be late.   _____

10   ⬭ = too easy   ☐ = too hard   △ = just right

Skill: Identifying repetition and redundancy

Making Tracks to Main Idea, © 1986 David S. Lake Publishers

Name _____

Circle the words in each passage that mean almost the same as the underlined word.

1. One of the most <u>sickening</u> things I ever saw was a glass of green milk. I think it is disgusting to change food color. Green milk is not appetizing. It is gross.

2. The ocean was <u>calm</u> after the storm. Peaceful waves rolled smoothly to the quiet shore. The water seemed restful at last.

3. The girls were very <u>hungry</u> after the hike. They had a large appetite for lunch. They said they were starving.

4. Many people <u>gathered</u> for the meeting. The interested men and women were grouped together only for a short time.

5. My <u>parents</u> are very hard working. My mother and father both have jobs. My folks never seem to stop and rest.

6. We need to be <u>polite</u>. It's a good idea to be respectful of other people. We can learn to be courteous.

⃝ = too easy   ☐ = too hard   △ = just right

11

Skill: Identifying repetition and redundancy

Name _____

Circle the words in each passage that mean almost the same as the underlined word or words.

1. I <u>enjoy</u> sports. I like baseball, football, and swimming. There are many other sports that I appreciate. Of all my interests, I care most about sports.

2. Bill <u>rushed</u> home from school because he didn't want to be late. As Bill hurried along, he checked the time. When he got home he was tired because he had run so far. Since he ran home from school, Bill arrived on time.

3. The wild dogs were <u>huge and dangerous</u>. They would attack unprotected sheep during the night. The large dogs were a menace because they might attack human beings. These gigantic dogs were threatening.

4. Gus <u>drowsed</u> during the television show. He fell asleep suddenly. We couldn't tell just when he dozed off.

5. Jane <u>inched</u> toward the top of the hill. She moved a small distance at a time. As she made tiny movements, she reached the summit.

6. I didn't understand the <u>plot</u> very well. The story was confusing, and I never figured out the plan.

12

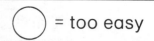 = too easy   □ = too hard   △ = just right

Skill: Identifying repetition and redundancy

Making Tracks to Main Idea, © 1986 David S. Lake Publishers

Name _____

List three words that fit each category.

1. tools used for measuring _____ _____ _____

2. needs of pets _____ _____ _____

3. people in a family _____ _____ _____

4. uses for wood _____ _____ _____

5. kinds of feelings _____ _____ _____

6. words beginning with Q _____ _____ _____

7. ways to cook _____ _____ _____

8. types of boats _____ _____ _____

9. kinds of music _____ _____ _____

10. names of cars _____ _____ _____

11. names of jobs _____ _____ _____

12. ways to travel _____ _____ _____

◯ = too easy ▢ = too hard △ = just right

13

Making Tracks to Main Idea, © 1986 David S. Lake Publishers

Skill: Determining relevance

Name _____

List three words that fit each category.

1. things to wear _____ _____ _____

2. things to read _____ _____ _____

3. animals that have feathers _____ _____ _____

4. tools for cleaning _____ _____ _____

5. objects colored purple _____ _____ _____

6. animals living in water _____ _____ _____

7. tools for cooking _____ _____ _____

8. kinds of paper _____ _____ _____

9. objects made from plastic _____ _____ _____

10. objects in the sky _____ _____ _____

11. needs for birthdays _____ _____ _____

12. medical supplies _____ _____ _____

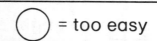

◯ = too easy   ▢ = too hard   △ = just right

Skill: Determining relevance

Making Tracks to Main Idea, © 1986 David S. Lake Publishers

Name _____

Underline the words in each sentence that tell **how.**

1. Please write carefully and clearly.

2. The man spoke distinctly.

3. Silently, the jaguar raced onward.

4. The ocean breeze blew gently and softly.

5. The treaty was agreed upon abruptly.

6. The cat killed the mouse noiselessly.

7. Susan climbed swiftly to the treetop.

8. With great precision, the surgeon started to work.

9. Throw the harpoon with strength and accuracy.

10. The teacher waited impatiently for the class to arrive.

11. Newspapers are printed steadily during the night.

12. Some tennis players accept decisions respectfully.

Making Tracks to Main Idea, © 1986 David S. Lake Publishers

◯ = too easy   ▭ = too hard   △ = just right

15

Skill: Determining relevance

Name _____

Underline the words in each sentence that tell **why.**

1. Kelly practiced soccer daily because she wanted to play well.

2. Address this letter carefully so that it will arrive on time.

3. Because they were invited to the party, Sandy and Pat were happy.

4. Morse code is useful for sending messages.

5. Wake up early tomorrow so we can get a quick start.

6. I will not watch television because I haven't finished my work.

7. She grinned foolishly because she was embarrassed by her mistake.

8. The old invention was put away because new machines were developed.

9. We watch television at 6:00 in order to see the news report.

10. Survival skills are needed if we are to live in the wilderness.

11. Save a little of what you earn so you can plan for the future.

12. Squirrels bury acorns so that they will have food for the winter.

16

◯ = too easy   ☐ = too hard   △ = just right

Skill: Determining relevance

Making Tracks to Main Idea, © 1986 David S. Lake Publishers

Name _____

Underline the words in each sentence that tell **who.**

1. The chattering squirrels ate their way through a pound of nuts.

2. An author must spend many hours developing an interesting plot.

3. The senior citizens were thrilled by the roller-coaster ride.

4. You must check on the campfire several times each night.

5. The captain of the team wasn't being fair.

6. You will succeed if you make enough of an effort.

7. The kittens were attracted by the saucers of milk.

8. Our family has owned a cabin for the past six years.

9. We have to hurry to reach the theater on time.

10. The driver bounced from side to side as his truck bumped along the road.

11. Some nasty pranksters were responsible for the damage.

12. I won't be in the race tomorrow.

◯ = too easy   ▢ = too hard   △ = just right

17

Skill: Determining relevance

Name _____

Complete each sentence. Fill in the blanks
to tell **when.**

1. She received a science kit _____ .

2. _____ we watched television.

3. They will all be coming _____ .

4. Did you listen to the radio _____ ?

5. _____ they hoped for sunny weather.

6. People lived in caves _____ .

7. We all jumped _____ .

8. The rattlesnake was coiled up _____ .

9. _____ he came out of the water.

10. We brushed our teeth _____ .

11. _____ the exciting event was over.

12. They can dance _____ .

 = too easy 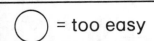 = too hard 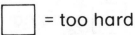 = just right

Name _____

Complete each sentence. Fill in the blanks
to tell **where.**

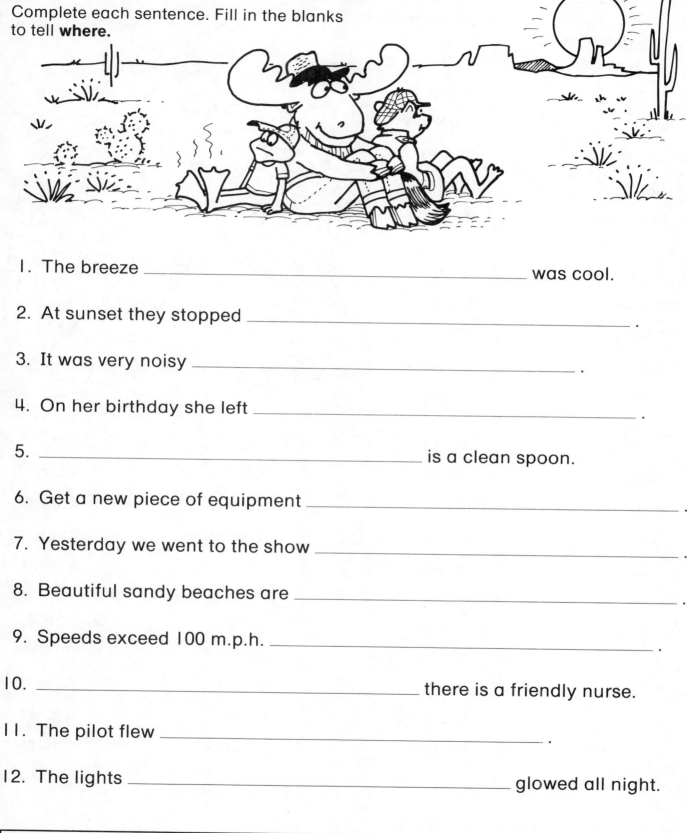

1. The breeze _____ was cool.

2. At sunset they stopped _____ .

3. It was very noisy _____ .

4. On her birthday she left _____ .

5. _____ is a clean spoon.

6. Get a new piece of equipment _____ .

7. Yesterday we went to the show _____ .

8. Beautiful sandy beaches are _____ .

9. Speeds exceed 100 m.p.h. _____ .

10. _____ there is a friendly nurse.

11. The pilot flew _____ .

12. The lights _____ glowed all night.

○ = too easy   ☐ = too hard   △ = just right

19

Making Tracks to Main Idea, © 1986 David S. Lake Publishers

Skill: Determining relevance

Name _____

Circle the word in each group that does not belong with the others.

1. hammer
   nails
   wood
   cloth
   saw

5. wood
   campfire
   match
   lighter
   torch

2. milk
   cheese
   apple
   butter
   cream

6. jelly
   bread
   jam
   honey
   syrup

3. wagon
   bike
   car
   wheelbarrow
   fence

7. house
   table
   bed
   chair
   stove

9. bag
   box
   envelope
   telephone
   folder

11. hat
    scarf
    mitten
    coat
    shovel

4. pilot
   jet
   rocket
   airplane
   helicopter

8. crayon
   pencil
   pen
   drawing
   brush

10. dime
    quarter
    dollar
    bank
    nickel

12. friend
    mother
    father
    uncle
    sister

20

 = too easy   ☐ = too hard   △ = just right

Skill: Classifying nouns

Making Tracks to Main Idea © 1986 David S. Lake Publishers

Name _____

Circle the word in each group that does not belong with the others.

1. kitchen
   bedroom
   fence
   porch
   hall

2. toad
   badger
   raccoon
   opossum
   fox

3. jacket
   shoes
   sweater
   parka
   coat

4. sequins
   necklace
   earring
   bracelet
   ring

5. clarinet
   trombone
   piano
   flute
   saxophone

6. jet
   rocket
   airplane
   helicopter
   bird

7. spool
   yarn
   string
   cord
   twine

8. dessert
   roll
   biscuit
   muffin
   bread

9. spider
   insect
   wasp
   mosquito
   allergy

10. cage
    zoo
    pen
    kennel
    jungle

11. chin
    temple
    knee
    forehead
    cheek

12. fence
    bush
    shrub
    hedge
    tree

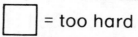 ◯ = too easy   ▢ = too hard   △ = just right

21

Skill: Classifying nouns

Name _____

Circle the activity in each group that does not belong with the others. Use a dictionary if you need help.

1. splashing
   floating
   swimming
   fishing

2. weeping
   moaning
   groaning
   humming

3. glittering
   shining
   glowing
   polishing

4. singing
   dancing
   acting
   reading

5. plunging
   running
   dipping
   diving

6. pitching
   batting
   catching
   pretending

7. longing
   buying
   wanting
   desiring

8. consuming
   devouring
   shopping
   eating

9. roasting
   baking
   chopping
   frying

10. resulting
    returning
    repaying
    restoring

11. stammering
    stuttering
    dozing
    faltering

12. agreeing
    arguing
    quarreling
    disputing

22

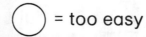 = too easy   ☐ = too hard   △ = just right

Skill: Classifying nouns

Making Tracks to Main Idea © 1996 David S. Lake Publishers

Name _____

Create a category for each group of activities. Write your answer on the line next to each group.

1. running
   kicking
   throwing _____

2. chewing
   munching
   swallowing _____

3. doodling
   sketching
   penciling _____

4. soaping
   rinsing
   drying _____

5. threading
   stitching
   knotting _____

6. sipping
   slurping
   swallowing _____

7. bending
   stooping
   stretching _____

8. showing
   training
   demonstrating _____

9. parting
   combing
   brushing _____

10. yelling
    singing
    humming _____

11. stomping
    kicking
    stamping _____

12. spending
    paying
    buying _____

◯ = too easy   ☐ = too hard   △ = just right

23

Skill: Classifying nouns

Name _____

List three nouns that fit each category.

1. vegetables

_____

_____

_____

2. foreign words

_____

_____

_____

3. sports equipment

_____

_____

_____

4. kinds of birds

_____

_____

_____

5. types of fish

_____

_____

_____

6. characters in fiction

_____

_____

_____

7. names of mountains

_____

_____

_____

8. states in the United States

_____

_____

_____

9. names of rivers

_____

_____

_____

10. names of U.S. presidents

_____

_____

_____

11. titles of books

_____

_____

_____

12. authors of books

_____

_____

_____

13. games

_____

_____

_____

14. poisons

_____

_____

_____

24

◯ = too easy   ▢ = too hard   △ = just right

Skill: Classifying nouns

Making Tracks to Main Idea, © 1986 David S. Lake Publishers

Name _____

List three nouns that fit each category.

1. tools for building

_____
_____
_____

2. items found in a bakery

_____
_____
_____

3. dairy products

_____
_____
_____

4. art supplies

_____
_____
_____

5. camping gear

_____
_____
_____

6. television shows

_____
_____
_____

7. names of girls

_____
_____
_____

8. kinds of stores

_____
_____
_____

9. things to read

_____
_____
_____

10. names of planets

_____
_____
_____

11. names of trees

_____
_____
_____

12. picnic supplies

_____
_____
_____

13. parts of a car

_____
_____
_____

14. large cities

_____
_____
_____

⬭ = too easy   ▢ = too hard   △ = just right

25

Skill: Classifying nouns

Name _____

List three nouns that fit each category.

1. warm clothing

_____

_____

_____

2. scientific equipment

_____

_____

_____

3. cartoon characters

_____

_____

_____

4. magazine titles

_____

_____

_____

5. types of art

_____

_____

_____

6. famous musicians

_____

_____

_____

7. names of sports teams

_____

_____

_____

8. large companies

_____

_____

_____

9. careers

_____

_____

_____

10. religions

_____

_____

_____

11. your friends

_____

_____

_____

12. clubs

_____

_____

_____

26 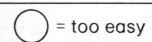 ◯ = too easy   ☐ = too hard   △ = just right

Skill: Classifying nouns

Name _____

List three nouns that fit each category.

1. refrigerated food

   _____
   _____
   _____

2. feelings

   _____
   _____
   _____

3. shoes in your closet

   _____
   _____
   _____

4. kinds of clothing

   _____
   _____
   _____

5. frightening things

   _____
   _____
   _____

6. comical characters

   _____
   _____
   _____

7. audio equipment

   _____
   _____
   _____

8. food on a menu

   _____
   _____
   _____

9. things in a museum

   _____
   _____
   _____

10. ads in a magazine

    _____
    _____
    _____

11. foreign languages

    _____
    _____
    _____

12. books teachers use

    _____
    _____
    _____

○ = too easy   □ = too hard   △ = just right

27

Making Tracks to Main Idea, © 1986 David S. Lake Publishers

Skill: Classifying nouns

Name _____

Complete each set of blanks with a list of items so each story makes sense. Then complete the last blank to explain how the listed items are related.

1. Young children like to play with small toys. Sometimes they use

   _____ , _____ , or _____ . Older children

   like to move around. They might like to play _____ ,

   _____ , or _____ .

   The listed items _____ .

2. The sky above us is really very crowded. In the sky last night I saw

   _____ , _____ , and _____ . Today,

   in the sunlit sky I saw _____ , _____ , and

   _____ . Maybe I'll even see a _____ or a

   _____ floating through the air.

   The listed items _____ .

3. If I were stranded on an island, I would most like to have _____ ,

   _____ , and _____ . Of course, in cold weather I

   might need _____ , _____ , or _____ .

   The listed items _____ .

4. Traveling is fun and exciting. I would take a train to go to

   _____ , _____ , or _____ . In an airplane I

   would go to _____ , _____ , or _____ . If

   I could travel in space, I would visit _____ or _____ .

   The listed items _____ .

28

◯ = too easy   ▢ = too hard   △ = just right

Skill: Classifying nouns

Making Tracks to Main Idea. © 1986 David S. Lake Publishers

Name _____

Complete each set of blanks with a list of items so each story makes sense. Then complete the last blank to explain how the listed items are related.

1. When we went to the mountains I packed _____ ,

   _____ , and _____ . Because it was expected to snow,

   I needed my _____ , _____ , and _____ .

   The listed items _____ .

2. This old car is falling apart. First the _____ , _____ ,

   and _____ broke. Then the _____ , _____ ,

   and _____ fell off.

   The listed items _____ .

3. In order to create the winning poster, I bought the best _____ ,

   _____ , and _____ to begin the job. Then I used

   _____ , _____ , and _____ to complete

   my poster. I won!

   The listed items _____ .

4. The best picnics are held on summer days. Some people like to eat

   _____ , _____ , and _____ . But I like to

   eat _____ , _____ and _____ when I'm

   outdoors.

   The listed items _____ .

Name _____

List three activities that fit each category.

1. running a race

   _____
   _____
   _____

2. camping in the woods

   _____
   _____
   _____

3. going to the moon

   _____
   _____
   _____

4. giving a present

   _____
   _____
   _____

5. receiving an award

   _____
   _____
   _____

6. reading a book

   _____
   _____
   _____

7. preparing a meal

   _____
   _____
   _____

8. building a house

   _____
   _____
   _____

9. comforting someone hurt

   _____
   _____
   _____

10. taking a photograph

    _____
    _____
    _____

11. driving a car

    _____
    _____
    _____

12. growing a garden

    _____
    _____
    _____

13. helping a friend

    _____
    _____
    _____

14. taking a nap

    _____
    _____
    _____

30

◯ = too easy   ▢ = too hard   △ = just right

Skill: Classifying series of events

Making Tracks to Main Idea © 1996 David S. Lake Publishers

Name _____

List three activities that fit each category.

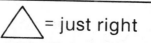

1. cooking

_____
_____
_____

2. playing tennis

_____
_____
_____

3. getting dressed

_____
_____
_____

4. shopping

_____
_____
_____

5. painting

_____
_____
_____

6. taking a trip

_____
_____
_____

7. telephoning

_____
_____
_____

8. getting a haircut

_____
_____
_____

9. borrowing a book

_____
_____
_____

10. washing windows

_____
_____
_____

11. going to school

_____
_____
_____

12. getting a job

_____
_____
_____

13. having a party

_____
_____
_____

14. writing a story

_____
_____
_____

◯ = too easy   ▢ = too hard   △ = just right

31

Skill: Classifying series of events

Name _____

List three activities that fit each category.

1. playing baseball

_____
_____
_____

2. buying clothing

_____
_____
_____

3. eating ice cream

_____
_____
_____

4. riding a horse

_____
_____
_____

5. having an adventure

_____
_____
_____

6. drawing a picture

_____
_____
_____

7. winning trophies

_____
_____
_____

8. paying bills

_____
_____
_____

9. solving mysteries

_____
_____
_____

10. writing poetry

_____
_____
_____

11. working with tools

_____
_____
_____

12. making music

_____
_____
_____

32

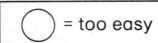 = too easy   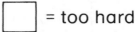 = too hard   △ = just right

Skill: Classifying series of events

Making Tracks to Main Idea © 1986 David S. Lake Publishers

Name _____

Read each passage to determine its topic.
Then fill in the blanks so the passage is
complete.

1. Larry _____ the plastic bag and took

   out two slices of bread. He _____ the

   top from a large jar of peanut butter. Larry

   _____ the peanut butter onto the bread

   with a knife. Then he _____ the jelly. At

   last, Larry _____ his sandwich.

2. The robot _____ the doorbell twice. When no one answered,

   it _____ the door and _____ right into the

   house. When it reached the kitchen, the robot _____ and

   _____ .

3. Some dinosaurs were extremely strong. They used their large size to

   _____ and _____ . Smaller animals could

   _____ and _____ , but they could not overcome

   the biggest dinosaurs.

4. In order to help around the house, Jerry was expected to _____ ,

   _____ , and _____ . It took him a long time to

   _____ and _____ . When he was finished, he planned

   to _____ and _____ with his friends.

⬭ = too easy   ☐ = too hard   △ = just right

33

Skill: Classifying series of events

Name _____

Read each passage to determine its topic.
Then fill in the blanks so the passage is
complete.

1. Once upon a time there was a clever magician. He

   learned to _____ and _____ .

   When he wanted to surprise people, the magician

   would _____ , _____ , and

   _____ . The townspeople really liked it

   when the magician would _____ and

   _____ .

2. On stormy days our school schedules unusual activities. The younger

   children spend time _____ , _____ , and

   _____ . Older students _____ , _____ ,

   and _____ . Even the teachers are happy to _____

   and _____ .

3. When Suzanne wanted to have a party, she knew she had a lot of work

   to do. To get ready, she had to _____ , _____ ,

   and _____ . Then, when her friends arrived, they could

   _____ , _____ , and _____ .

4. Hardworking students are those who _____ , _____ ,

   and _____ in class. They use their time well at home as they

   _____ and _____ .

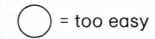 = too easy $\square$ = too hard    = just right

Skill: Classifying series of events

Making Tracks to Main Idea © 1996 David S. Lake Publishers

Name _____

Draw a picture to illustrate each of the following passages. Under each picture, copy the sentence that best explains the passage.

1. Leprechauns are small, imaginary people. They wear green clothes and live in Ireland. Supposedly, leprechauns know how to find a big pot of gold at the end of a rainbow.

_____

2. I had a hard time waking up this morning. My alarm clock rang, my dad called me, and my dog jumped on the bed. Finally, I smelled breakfast, and I got up in a hurry.

_____

◯ = too easy   ▢ = too hard   △ = just right

35

Skill: Identifying topic sentences

Name _____

Draw a picture to illustrate each of the following passages. Under each picture, copy the sentence that best explains the passage.

1. Benjamin Franklin was an interesting, famous American. He was one of the men who helped create the United States of America. He also produced inventions. Franklin is most famous for an experiment with a kite, a key, and lightning.

2. Wild animal hunters often go to jungles, deserts, and wildlife areas. They take cameras, camping gear, and weapons. Sometimes they kill animals for meat, skins, or fur. Other times they observe and photograph the animals they see.

36 ◯ = too easy ▢ = too hard △ = just right

Skill: Identifying topic sentences

Making Tracks to Main Idea, © 1986 David S. Lake Publishers

Name _____

Write a sentence to describe each of the following:

1. a new electronic game _____
_____

2. a meal in a restaurant _____
_____

3. a room in your home _____
_____

4. an interesting dream _____
_____

5. a winter vacation _____
_____

6. your chance on a TV game show _____
_____

7. a newspaper story _____
_____

8. an accident _____
_____

◯ = too easy　　☐ = too hard　　△ = just right

37

Skill: Inventing topic sentences

Name _____

Write a sentence to tell how the words in each group are related.

1. prancing

   trotting

   galloping _____

2. space

   rocket

   planet _____

3. tornado

   hurricane

   thunderstorm _____

4. doctor

   minister

   lawyer _____

5. writing

   addressing

   mailing _____

38 ⬤ = too easy   ▢ = too hard   △ = just right

Skill: Inventing topic sentences

Making Tracks to Main Idea © 1986 David S. Lake Publishers

Name _____

Write a sentence to describe each of the following:

1. the best present you ever gave _____

_____

2. your earliest memory _____

_____

3. your dream house _____

_____

4. an ocean voyage _____

_____

5. physical fitness _____

_____

6. your favorite vacation _____

_____

7. your closest friends _____

_____

8. your favorite reading material _____

_____

40

◯ = too easy   ▢ = too hard   △ = just right

Skill: Inventing topic sentences

Making Tracks to Main Idea, © 1986 David S. Lake Publishers

Name _____

Write a sentence to tell how the words in each group are related.

1. mix

   bake

   eat _____

2. pack

   carry

   move _____

3. read

   write

   draw _____

4. hear

   see

   feel _____

5. jump

   skip

   hop _____

6. Mexico

   France

   Japan _____

◯ = too easy   ☐ = too hard   △ = just right

39

Skill: Inventing topic sentences

Name _____

Write a topic sentence for each story idea.
Include at least four of the following in each
sentence: **who, what, where, when, why,** and **how.**

1. Disneyland _____

_____

_____

2. wild animals _____

_____

_____

3. magic _____

_____

_____

4. babies _____

_____

_____

5. sports _____

_____

_____

6. space discoveries _____

_____

_____

7. sickness _____

_____

_____

8. talent _____

_____

_____

Making Tracks to Main Idea, © 1986 David S. Lake Publishers

◯ = too easy　　☐ = too hard　　△ = just right

41

Skill: Inventing topic sentences

Name _____

Write a topic sentence for each story idea.
Include at least four of the following in each
sentence: **who, what, where, when, why,** and **how.**

1. happiness _____
_____
_____

2. growing up _____
_____
_____

3. school _____
_____
_____

4. weather _____
_____
_____

5. famous people _____
_____
_____

6. forests _____
_____
_____

7. flying _____
_____
_____

8. the old days _____
_____
_____

42 ⬭ = too easy   ▢ = too hard   △ = just right

Skill: Inventing topic sentences

Making Tracks to Main Idea, © 1986 David S. Lake Publishers

Name _____

Write a topic sentence for each story idea.
Include at least four of the following in each
sentence: **who, what, where, when, why,** and **how.**

1. submarines _____
_____
_____

2. birthdays _____
_____
_____

3. travel _____
_____
_____

4. comic books _____
_____
_____

5. family life _____
_____
_____

6. bridges _____
_____
_____

7. jokes _____
_____
_____

8. clouds _____
_____
_____

◯ = too easy   ☐ = too hard   △ = just right   **43**

Skill: Inventing topic sentences

Name _____

Write a topic sentence for each story idea.
Include at least four of the following in each
sentence: **who, what, where, when, why,** and **how.**

1. skyscrapers _____

_____

_____

2. electronic games _____

_____

_____

3. an award _____

_____

_____

4. summertime _____

_____

_____

5. friends _____

_____

_____

6. working _____

_____

_____

7. food _____

_____

_____

8. animals _____

_____

_____

44 ⬭ = too easy   ☐ = too hard   △ = just right

Skill: Inventing topic sentences

Making Tracks to Main Idea, © 1986 David S. Lake Publishers

_____

e the best main idea for each

dy tossed in his sleep as he dreamed of the
rightening moment of his life. Once again he
one on the beach, hearing the ocean sound that
ild not forget. The giant waves settled down
fully on the sand, but nowhere could he find his
/.

   a. The waves are big, but they are not dangerous.

   b. Teddy doesn't enjoy his trips to the beach.

   c. Teddy has nightmares about being alone.

2. The workers pulled into the driveway of the nearly completed apartment building. Carefully checking the straps of their climbing gear, they prepared to climb the wall of the building. They used narrow grippers for finger- and toeholds. Once they passed the sixth floor, they looked like toy people to the viewers below.

   a. It is very dangerous to climb without safety gear.

   b. Someone is playing with toy people on the roof.

   c. Workers are climbing a building to complete construction.

Making Tracks to Main Idea, © 1986 David S. Lake Publishers

◯ = too easy   ▢ = too hard   △ = just right

45

Skill: Identifying main idea

Name _____

Underline the best main idea for each passage.

1. When the rains come in February, the creeks flow again and the grass turns green. Large salamanders crawl out in the mud, and sometimes they sun themselves on the road. At night you can hear frogs croaking by the riverbank and crickets chirping in the ferns. The air smells moist at this time of the year.

   a. Salamanders enjoy playing in the mud and on the road.

   b. If the creeks do not have water, the small animals will die.

   c. The rains in February refresh the earth and bring out small animals.

2. When Marigold was a baby, she was as cute as a button. Everyone hugged and petted her and told her how cuddly and warm she was. Marigold was happy to be so loved. But as she grew older, she grew fat. Marigold played in the mud, and her skin turned hard and cracked. Marigold was not cute anymore, and she began to smell. No one wanted to hug her or touch her. In fact, the only person who even looked at her with pleasure was Mr. Durk, the hog butcher.

   a. Pigs can be cute as babies, but they are mostly appreciated for their meat.

   b. Babies need love and a good diet to be attractive.

   c. Mr. Durk wanted Marigold for a pet.

46

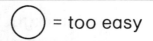 = too easy   ☐ = too hard   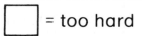 = just right

Skill: Identifying main idea

Name _____

Underline the best main idea for each passage.

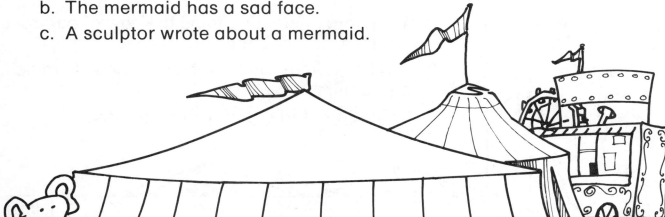

1. Last week, when the circus came to town, all the children wanted to see the show. The huge tent was put up on Harrison's vacant lot, and the circus people parked their campers along the side of Main Street. This group had twelve tigers and seven elephants, many more than we had ever seen at one time. The only disappointing part of the show was the clowns, who weren't particularly funny.

   a. Circus people travel in campers.

   b. The circus came to town last week.

   c. My favorite part of the circus was the clowns.

2. There is a statue in Copenhagen called "The Little Mermaid." This statue is made of bronze. The sculptor who made this statue based it on the story of a little mermaid whose heart was broken when the man she loved decided to marry a woman. The statue is placed in the harbor where visitors can see it easily.

   a. "The Little Mermaid" is a statue in Copenhagen.

   b. The mermaid has a sad face.

   c. A sculptor wrote about a mermaid.

◯ = too easy	▢ = too hard	△ = just right

47

Making Tracks to Main Idea, © 1986 David S. Lake Publishers

Skill: Identifying main idea

Name _____

Underline the best main idea for each passage.

1. Some of the larger zoos in the world have small ponds or lakes designed especially for keeping birds on display in a natural environment. A bird pond will attract local birds and is a comfortable home for rare and exotic birds, too. In order to keep the birds in the zoo, the zookeepers sometimes pinion the birds' wings. This means that they clip the tip of one wing, throwing off the bird's balance so that it cannot fly away.

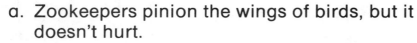

   a. Zookeepers pinion the wings of birds, but it doesn't hurt.

   b. Zoos use natural and artificial ways to keep birds on display.

   c. Zoos must build ponds or lakes to keep birds happy.

2. Trolls, gnomes, and hobbits are characters in some of the best stories written for children. These small, ugly creatures can be either villains or heroes. It is interesting to notice that they are almost always male. Have you ever read a story with a female troll, gnome, or hobbit in it?

   a. There are interesting facts to know about trolls, gnomes, and hobbits.

   b. Trolls, gnomes, and hobbits are usually male characters.

   c. Children's stories are written for boys.

48

◯ = too easy   ☐ = too hard   △ = just right

Skill: Identifying main idea

Making Tracks to Main Idea © 1986 David S. Lake Publishers

Name _____

Underline the best main idea for each passage.

1. Rotating slowly above the auditorium, the fan moved the stale air lazily from one end of the room to another. The speaker's voice was soft and low. A sense of relaxation settled over me, and I found it difficult to keep my eyes from closing.

   a. The speaker was boring.

   b. A quiet speaker in a stuffy room can put me to sleep.

   c. Smoking should not be allowed in public places.

2. Red and green lights twinkled through the branches of a huge pine tree. Small toys hung from golden cords on each twig, and silver tinsel sparkled and dripped from the needles. Scattered among the decorations, popcorn balls and cinnamon sticks gave off a delicious odor. A small child climbed carefully to the top of a ladder and reached over to place a shining star on the very top of the tree.

   a. Christmas is a wonderful time of year.

   b. Children decorated a tree.

   c. A tree has been decorated for celebration.

◯ = too easy   ▢ = too hard   △ = just right

49

Skill: Identifying main idea

Name _____

For each passage, underline the sentence that best states the main idea.

1. A hungry stranger arrived at a farmhouse late in the day. When he found that no one was home, he twisted the lock, turned the knob, and opened the door. In the kitchen he ate bread, cheese, and fruit. Then he wrote a message, carefully closed the door, and walked down the road.

   a. A hungry stranger broke into an empty house to get food.

   b. A locked door was opened in a hurry.

   c. Always write a thank-you note when you take something.

2. John enjoys watching movies that have plenty of action, excitement, and danger. He often goes to the movie theater to see westerns, war pictures, and detective stories. At home, he watches spy movies and animal adventures on television.

   a. Westerns, spy stories, and animal adventures are dangerous.

   b. War movies are full of action and danger.

   c. John watches many exciting movies.

3. At school we work hard most of the day. We read, write, and listen. Sometimes we have tests, or quizzes. Other times we write reports, work on projects, and finish art assignments.

   a. School is lots of fun.

   b. At school we do many kinds of work.

   c. Tests are hard work at school.

50

 ◯ = too easy   ▢ = too hard   △ = just right

Skill: Identifying main idea

Making Tracks to Main Idea, © 1986 David S. Lake Publishers

Name _____

For each passage, underline the sentence
that best states the main idea.

1. The midnight rain stopped, leaving the house quiet
with only the echoes of dripping water. It was cold in
the dark, empty building, and the inspector shivered
as she kept watch for the mysterious trespasser.

    a. A detective is staking out a house at night.

    b. Empty houses are scary at night.

    c. Someone is trespassing in the rain.

2. Do you know what the words "white water" mean?
To a river rafter, they mean excitement and danger.
When water passes quickly over rocks or logs, it
churns up waves that are white with foam. The waves
might toss a raft several feet into the air. If a raft is
turned over by white water, the passengers are in
trouble!

    a. River rafting is dangerous in white water.

    b. White water churns over rocks and logs where
       people ride rafts.

    c. River rafters should watch for rough white water.

3. Lee packed her small suitcase hurriedly, grabbed
her coat, bounded down the stairs, and ran out the
door. Running to the corner, she shouted and waved
to the taxi that was always parked in front of the
doughnut shop. The driver heard her call, started the
engine, and pulled to the curb so Lee could scramble
into the car. "Take me to the airport, and hurry
please!" Lee gasped.

    a. Lee rides taxis and eats doughnuts often.

    b. The taxi driver knows where to park to find
       riders.

    c. Lee is taking a trip in a hurry.

Making Tracks to Main Idea, © 1986 David S. Lake Publishers

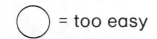 = too easy   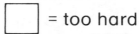 = too hard   △ = just right

51

Skill: Identifying main idea

Name _____

Match each title to its correct meaning. Use each title only once. Write the title on the line next to its meaning.

captain   Mrs.

chairperson   officer

maestro   president

Mr.   reverend

Senator   Sir

1. a married woman _____

2. a member of the clergy _____

3. a member of the police force _____

4. a member of the Senate _____

5. a symphony conductor _____

6. an adult man _____

7. a leader of a team _____

8. a director of a meeting _____

9. a leader of a country _____

10. a knight _____

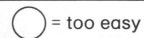 = too easy   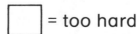 = too hard   △ = just right

Skill: Understanding and using titles

Making Tracks to Main Idea, © 1986 David S. Lake Publishers

Name _____

Create an imaginary title for each of the
following:

1. a comedy play _____

2. a plastic toy _____

3. your reading class _____

4. your autobiography _____

5. a secondhand shop _____

6. the person in charge of paper clips _____

7. bottled lemonade _____

8. a love poem _____

9. a nature guide _____

10. a reading comprehension workbook _____

11. a song for a rock star _____

12. a famous orchestra _____

13. your playground _____

14. your school cafeteria _____

15. an imaginary pet _____

16. your own zoo _____

◯ = too easy   ▢ = too hard   △ = just right

53

Skill: Understanding and using titles

Name _____

Create an imaginary title for each of the
following:

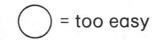

1. a newspaper _____

2. a magazine _____

3. a mystery story _____

4. a TV adventure series _____

5. a horror movie _____

6. a photograph of yourself _____

7. a school for smart persons _____

8. a reading club _____

9. a new job _____

10. a book of jokes _____

11. a cookbook _____

12. a cartoon strip _____

13. a leader of another planet _____

14. a new invention _____

15. a drawing of your new home _____

16. a new song _____

54

| ⬭ = too easy | ☐ = too hard | △ = just right |

Skill: Understanding and using titles

Making Tracks to Main Idea © 1986 David S. Lake Publishers

Name _____

Write three sentences that fit each book title.

Growing Up

1. _____
_____
_____
_____
_____
_____
_____

Adventure at Sea

2. _____
_____
_____
_____
_____
_____
_____

Detective Mystery

3. _____
_____
_____
_____
_____
_____
_____

| ◯ = too easy | ▢ = too hard | △ = just right | **55** |

Making Tracks to Main Idea, © 1986 David S. Lake Publishers

Skill: Understanding and using titles

Name _____

Write three sentences that fit each book title.

Best Jokes!

1. _____
_____
_____
_____
_____

Being Smart

2. _____
_____
_____
_____
_____

Fast Food for Me!

3. _____
_____
_____
_____
_____

56

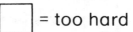

◯ = too easy   ☐ = too hard   △ = just right

Skill: Understanding and using titles

Making Tracks to Main Idea © 1986 David S. Lake Publishers

Name _____

Write three sentences that fit each book title.

Games

1. _____

_____

_____

_____

_____

_____

Poetry

2. _____

_____

_____

_____

_____

_____

American History

3. _____

_____

_____

_____

_____

_____

Making Tracks to Main Idea, © 1986 David S. Lake Publishers

◯ = too easy   ▢ = too hard   △ = just right

57

Name _____

Write three sentences that fit each book title.

**The Great
Space
Race**

I. _____
_____
_____
_____
_____
_____

**Tales of
Great
Feats**

2. _____
_____
_____
_____
_____
_____

**Animal
Antics**

3. _____
_____
_____
_____
_____
_____

58

 = too easy   ☐ = too hard   △ = just right

Skill: Understanding and using titles

Making Tracks to Main Idea, © 1986 David S. Lake Publishers

Answer Key

Page 7

The following words should be circled:
1. enjoy, 2. huge, 3. award, 4. banquet, 5. shore, 6. faith, 7. curve, 8. burst, 9. mistake, 10. persons, 11. squeeze, 12. sturdy, 13. young, 14. summit, 15. reject, 16. weak, 17. deluge, 18. plenty, 19. invention, 20. confer, 21. restrain, 22. thorough, 23. reply, 24. wrath, 25. change, 26. loving, 27. liquid, 28. schedule, 29. sacred, 30. rural, 31. wealthy, 32. usual, 33. join, 34. old, 35. awkward, 36. hide

Page 8

The following words should be circled:
1. pursue, 2. guide, 3. refuse, 4. destroy, 5. change, 6. timid, 7. theme, 8. laugh, 9. skillful, 10. gloomy, 11. deceive, 12. boast, 13. transmit, 14. known, 15. truth, 16. calm, 17. elevate, 18. faith, 19. commend, 20. horrible, 21. fight, 22. weigh, 23. overlook, 24. strange, 25. complete, 26. sickly, 27. find, 28. decrease, 29. falsehood, 30. crazy, 31. noisy, 32. mostly, 33. cover, 34. midst, 35. force, 36. award

Page 9

Accept appropriate synonyms.

Page 10

Accept appropriate synonyms.

Page 11

The following words should be circled (accept appropriate variations):
1. disgusting, not appetizing, gross; 2. peaceful, rolled smoothly, quiet, restful; 3. large appetite, starving; 4. were grouped together; 5. mother and father, folks· 6. respectful, courteous

Page 12

The following words should be circled (accept appropriate variations):
1. like, appreciate, care most about; 2. hurried, had run, ran; 3. large, were a menace, gigantic, threatening; 4. fell asleep, dozed off; 5. moved a small· distance, made tiny movements; 6. story, plan

Page 13

Accept appropriate responses.

Page 14

Accept appropriate responses.

Page 15

The following words should be underlined:

1. carefully and clearly, 2. distinctly, 3. Silently, 4. gently and softly, 5. abruptly, 6. noiselessly, 7. swiftly, 8. With great precision, 9. with strength and accuracy, 10. impatiently, 11. steadily, 12. respectfully

Page 16

The following words should be underlined:

1. because she wanted to play well, 2. so that it will arrive on time, 3. Because they were invited to the party, 4. for sending messages, 5. so we can get a quick start, 6. because I haven't finished my work, 7. because she was embarrassed by her mistake, 8. because new machines were developed, 9. in order to see the news report, 10. if we are to live in the wilderness, 11. so you can plan for the future, 12. so that they will have food for the winter

Page 17

The following words should be underlined:

1. The chattering squirrels, 2. An author, 3. The senior citizens, 4. You, 5. The captain of the team, 6. You, 7. The kittens, 8. Our family, 9. We, 10. The driver, 11. Some nasty pranksters, 12. I

Page 18

Accept appropriate responses that tell when.

Page 19

Accept appropriate responses that tell where.

Page 20

The following words should be circled:

1. cloth, 2. apple, 3. fence, 4. pilot, 5. wood, 6. bread, 7. house, 8. drawing, 9. telephone, 10. bank, 11. shovel, 12. friend

Page 21

The following words should be circled:

1. fence, 2. toad, 3. shoes, 4. sequins, 5. piano, 6. bird, 7. spool, 8. dessert, 9. allergy, 10. jungle, 11. knee, 12. fence

Page 22

The following words should be circled:

1. fishing, 2. humming, 3. polishing, 4. reading, 5. running, 6. pretending, 7. buying, 8. shopping, 9. chopping, 10. resulting, 11. dozing, 12. agreeing

Page 23

Accept variations of the following:

1. playing ball, 2. eating, 3. drawing, 4. washing, 5. sewing, 6. drinking, 7. exercising, 8. teaching, 9. styling hair, 10. vocalizing, 11. moving feet, 12. shopping

Page 24

Accept appropriate nouns.

Page 25

Accept appropriate nouns.

Page 26

Accept appropriate nouns.

Page 27

Accept appropriate nouns.

Page 28

Accept appropriate groups of words.

Page 29

Accept appropriate groups of words.

Page 30

Accept appropriate activities.

Page 31

Accept appropriate activities.

Page 32

Accept appropriate activities.

Making Tracks to Main Idea © 1986 David S. Lake Publishers

Page 33
Accept appropriate responses.

Page 34
Accept appropriate responses.

Page 35
Accept appropriate pictures and topic sentences.

Page 36
Accept appropriate pictures and topic sentences.

Page 37
Accept appropriate responses.

Page 38
Accept appropriate responses.

Page 39
Accept appropriate responses.

Page 40
Accept appropriate responses.

Page 41
Accept appropriate responses.

Page 42
Accept appropriate responses.

Page 43
Accept appropriate responses.

Page 44
Accept appropriate responses.

Page 45
1. c, 2. c

Page 46
1. c, 2. a

Page 47
1. b, 2. a

Page 48
1. b, 2. a

Page 49
1. b, 2. c

Page 50
1. a, 2. c, 3. b

Page 51
1. a, 2. a or c, 3. c

Page 52
1. Mrs., 2. reverend, 3. officer, 4. Senator, 5. maestro, 6. Mr., 7. captain, 8. chairperson, 9. president, 10. Sir

Page 53
Accept appropriate responses.

Page 54
Accept appropriate responses.

Page 55
Accept appropriate responses.

Page 56
Accept appropriate responses.

Page 57
Accept appropriate responses.

Page 58
Accept appropriate responses.

Part II

Inferences

Making Inferences

Grades 1–3

Contents

Introduction

The lessons in this workbook develop eight subskills for making inferences. The reproducible worksheets are organized into sections, each section pertaining to one of the eight subskills:

1. **Finding Sequence Clues**
2. **Using Descriptive Language**
3. **Clarifying Vocabulary**
4. **Relating Text to Experience**
5. **Visualizing**
6. **Understanding Point of View**
7. **Inventing Alternatives**
8. **Predicting Consequences and Conclusions**

At the conclusion of each activity is an evaluation code box.

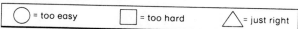

An evaluation of item difficulty can be made by enclosing the item number within one of the shapes shown in the box to relay the coded message. Another way to use the code box is simply to shade in the shape that best evaluates the page. This evaluation might be made by the teacher, the student, a tutor, or a team. The code is designed to help determine skill areas needing further attention.

The following section suggests additional activities for continued practice in making inferences.

Additional Activities

1. Who Said It?
Read a statement, such as "We will be constructing a ten-story building." Then ask students, "Who said it?" Give them a choice of three responses (soldier, dentist, engineer).

2. Silly Sentences
Change a noun in a sentence to make an absurd statement. Explain the absurdity. For example: We traveled on a *train* for miles (change *train* to *basketball, mouse,* or *coat hanger*).

3. Reading Melodrama

Write a response word on a card for each character in a story. Read the story orally. Each time a character is named, have some students hold up the response card for the character while the other students respond vocally. For example: Johnny Tremain yeah! was horrified to see his wealthy uncle boo! .

4. Comic Completion

Collect comic strips and cut off the last frame of each. Have readers select strips, write their own conclusions, and draw pictures to complete the strips.

5. Character Horoscopes

Have readers collect information about the qualities of people born under the different zodiac signs. Then use the information to try to identify the signs of book or story characters.

6. Story Continuation

Ask students to read the last paragraph or page of a story. Then have them write an additional ending to explain what happened after the original story ending took place.

7. Predictions

Read a story to a preselected point. Then have readers make individual predictions for the subsequent course of events. When the reading is completed, compare the actual ending with those predicted. Discuss how the story would have been different if the predictions had actually happened.

8. Visual Sequencing

As students read or listen to a story, have them illustrate major events. This is more effective if the drawing paper is divided into numbered squares and drawings are kept simple.

9. Read Together

Have students read the words they know from selected reading material, while the teacher or teacher aide reads the difficult words. Select recipes, advertisements, mail, newspapers, comics, weather predictions, labels, directions, or other common printed matter. Discuss the meanings of interesting words. Read together regularly and casually. (Not all reading needs to be formal.)

10. Television

Ask questions about the television programs which the students have viewed. Share opinions and feelings. Retell stories or shows, and practice creating different outcomes.

Name _____

Draw three pictures to tell a story about each topic.

1. **The Best Birthday**

First

Then

At last

2. **How to Be Happy**

First

Then

At last

3. **When the Puppy Was Hurt**

First

Then

At last

◯ = too easy   ☐ = too hard   △ = just right

7

Skill: Finding sequence clues

Name _____

Draw three pictures to tell a story about each topic.

1. Cooking Dinner

First

Then

At last

2. Making a Castle

First

Then

At last

3. Giving a Present

First

Then

At last

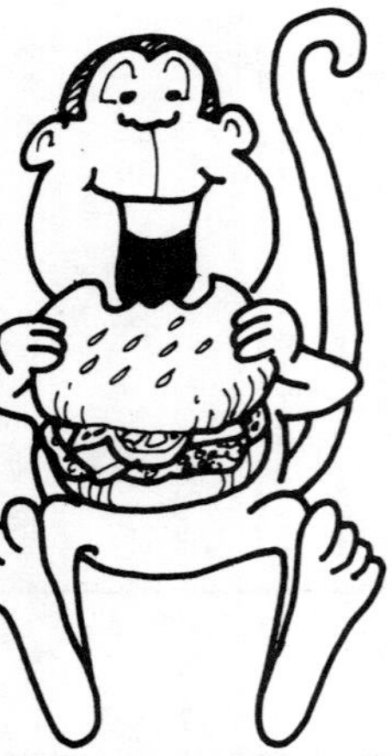

8

⃝ = too easy   ▢ = too hard   △ = just right

Skill: Finding sequence clues

Name _____

Draw three pictures to tell a story about each topic.

1. **Magic Tricks**

First	Then	At last

2. **Zoo Animals**

First	Then	At last

3. **Fast Cars**

First	Then	At last

Making Inferences, © 1986 David S. Lake Publishers

◯ = too easy   ▢ = too hard   △ = just right

9

Name _____

Draw three pictures to tell a story about each topic.

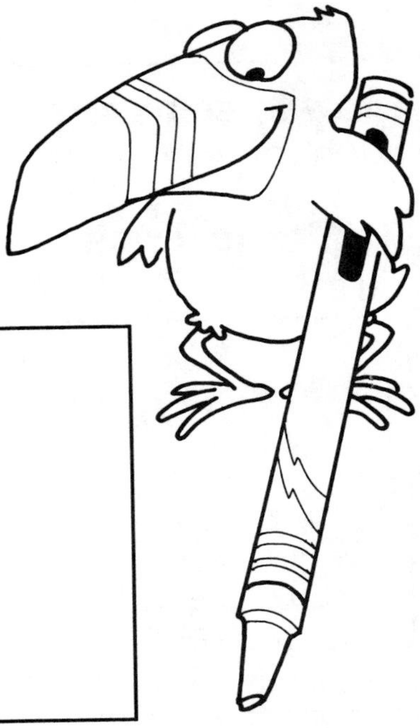

1. A Tasty Meal

First

Then

At last

2. A Funny Movie

First

Then

At last

3. An Old Cat

First

Then

At last

10

◯ = too easy   ▢ = too hard   △ = just right

Skill: Finding sequence clues

Making Inferences. © 1986 David S. Lake Publishers

Fill in the blanks to complete each story.

1. When I was small, I _____

   _____ .

   As I grew older, I _____

   _____ .

   Now I always _____

   _____ .

2. Do you remember _____ ?

   Many people used to _____ .

   I wonder if we'll ever _____ .

3. When the puppy was little, _____ .

   Now he can _____ .

   Soon he will _____ .

4. Before I opened the box, _____ .

   After _____ .

   Then _____ .

◯ = too easy   ▢ = too hard   △ = just right   **11**

Skill: Finding sequence clues

Name _____

Fill in the blanks to complete each story.

1. Once upon a time, there was a _____ .

   This _____ wanted to _____ .

   First _____ .

   Then _____ .

   At last _____ .

2. Last summer I _____ .

   Now I _____ .

   Next year I will _____ .

3. We always wanted to _____ .

   Then one day _____ .

   Finally _____ .

4. Long ago, people used to _____ .

   Then they invented _____ .

   Now people can _____ .

12

○ = too easy   □ = too hard   △ = just right

Skill: Finding sequence clues

Making Inferences, © 1986 David S. Lake Publishers

Name _____

Read each sentence. Think about what happened first and what happened second. Write the words that tell what happened **first.**

1. There was a big snowfall, and the roof fell in.

   _____

2. Before we could start the fire, we looked for wood.

   _____

3. Once we made ice cream. It really tasted good!

   _____

4. Sue went to a party, and it was late when she came home.

   _____

5. We mixed sugar and butter so we could make cookies.

   _____

6. The princess lived happily after she married the prince.

   _____

◯ = too easy   ▢ = too hard   △ = just right

13

Skill: Finding sequence clues

Name _____

Read each sentence. Think about what happened first and what happened second. Write the words that tell what happened **second.**

1. When Joe fell down, he cried.

_____

2. Jenny wanted a pet. Finally she got a dog.

_____

3. After I had waited for months, my birthday arrived.

_____

4. First we found a bowl. Then we mixed the batter.

_____

5. We went inside after the storm came.

_____

6. He had to wait for such a long time. Finally he opened the present.

_____

14

| 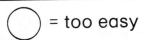 = too easy | ☐ = too hard | △ = just right |

Skill: Finding sequence clues

Making Inferences, © 1986 David S. Lake Publishers

Name _____

Write three words that tell more about each set of words below.

1. that _____ man

   _____

   _____

2. six _____ people

   _____

   _____

3. your _____ desk

   _____

   _____

4. this _____ smell

   _____

   _____

5. some _____ frogs

   _____

   _____

6. four _____ dogs

   _____

   _____

7. this _____ road

   _____

   _____

8. that _____ park

   _____

   _____

9. this _____ school

   _____

   _____

10. these _____ workers

   _____

   _____

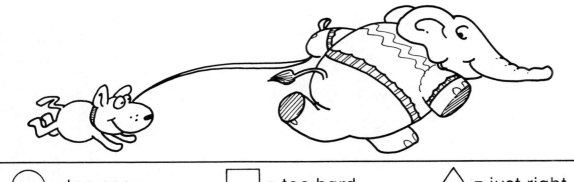

◯ = too easy   ☐ = too hard   △ = just right

15

Skill: Using descriptive language

Name _____

Write three words that tell more about
each set of words below.

1. this _____ book

_____

_____

2. those _____ flowers

_____

_____

3. our _____ teacher

_____

_____

7. these _____ cars

_____

_____

4. that _____ monkey

_____

_____

8. this _____ movie

_____

_____

5. many _____ snakes

_____

_____

9. this _____ mountain

_____

_____

6. that _____ room

_____

_____

10. three _____ bags

_____

_____

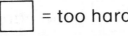

16

⬭ = too easy   ▢ = too hard   △ = just right

Skill: Using descriptive language

Making Inferences, © 1986 David S. Lake Publishers

Name _____

Fill in the blanks to tell **how.**

1. She sang a song _____

   _____ .

2. I ate my lunch _____

   _____ .

3. Please walk home _____

   _____ .

4. We _____ ran to the water.

5. Sometimes I run _____ .

6. He ate the sandwich _____ .

7. You write stories _____ .

8. Let's dig this hole _____ .

9. Ann _____ rode her bike home.

10. The baby _____ learned to walk.

◯ = too easy   ▢ = too hard   △ = just right

17

Skill: Using descriptive language

Name _____

Draw a picture of each item. Then write three words to tell more about the item in each of your pictures.

1. a witch

_____ , _____ , _____

2. a jet

_____ , _____ , _____

3. a shark

_____ , _____ , _____

18

○ = too easy   □ = too hard   △ = just right

Skill: Using descriptive language

Making Inferences, © 1986 David S. Lake Publishers

Draw a picture of each item. Then write three words to tell more about the item in each of your pictures.

1. a scarecrow

_____ , _____ , _____

2. a peanut-butter sandwich

_____ , _____ , _____

3. a dinosaur

_____ , _____ , _____

◯ = too easy   ▢ = too hard   △ = just right

19

Skill: Using descriptive language

Name _____

Fill in the blanks to make each sentence tell more about its topic. Then draw a picture to go with each sentence.

1. My friend is _____ , _____ , and _____ .

2. My house is _____ , _____ , and _____ .

3. My school is _____ , _____ , and _____ .

20

◯ = too easy   ▢ = too hard   △ = just right

Skill: Using descriptive language

Name _____

Make descriptive sentences. Use words from the box to complete the sentences below.

bulldozer	mop
dinosaur	peanut
flagpole	snail
goose	worm
hippopotamus	zebra

1. I eat like a _____ .

2. Don't run like a _____ .

3. He worked like a _____ .

4. She sang like a _____ .

5. My hair looks like a _____ .

6. It is the same size as a _____ .

7. He is as tall as a _____ .

8. You are as fast as a _____ .

9. Let me go as high as a _____ .

10. Don't move like a _____ .

Draw a picture of your funniest sentence.

◯ = too easy	▢ = too hard	△ = just right

21

Skill: Using descriptive language

Name _____

Name three things that can be:

1. fast   _____
   _____
   _____

2. tall   _____
   _____
   _____

3. black   _____
   _____
   _____

4. pretty   _____
   _____
   _____

5. smart   _____
   _____
   _____

6. funny   _____
   _____
   _____

7. round   _____
   _____
   _____

8. flat   _____
   _____
   _____

9. wrinkled   _____
   _____
   _____

10. wet   _____
   _____
   _____

22

◯ = too easy   ▢ = too hard   △ = just right

Skill: Clarifying vocabulary

Name _____

Name three things that can be:

1. used for
   eating
   _____
   _____
   _____

2. under the
   ground
   _____
   _____
   _____

3. used to
   keep
   warm
   _____
   _____
   _____

4. next to
   a tree
   _____
   _____
   _____

5. used in
   school
   _____
   _____
   _____

6. under a
   table
   _____
   _____
   _____

7. in a
   toolbox
   _____
   _____
   _____

8. used for
   fun
   _____
   _____
   _____

9. in outer
   space
   _____
   _____
   _____

10. next to
    a house
    _____
    _____
    _____

○ = too easy   □ = too hard   △ = just right

23

Name _____

Circle the word that means the **opposite** of the word in dark type.

1. **happy**   merry   gloomy

2. **ugly**   pretty   dirty

3. **glad**   sad   nice

4. **clever**   smart   stupid

5. **hide**   seek   cover

6. **float**   sink   swim

7. **build**   destroy   draw

8. **shut**   close   open

9. **melt**   soften   harden

10. **many**   few   all

11. **best**   good   worst

12. **find**   need   lose

24   ◯ = too easy   ▢ = too hard   △ = just right

Skill: Clarifying vocabulary

Name _____

Circle the word that means the **opposite**
of the word in dark type.

1. **past**   morning   future

2. **always**   never   often

3. **sick**   ill   well

4. **save**   spend   give

5. **over**   past   under

6. **noon**   midnight   lunchtime

7. **give**   want   take

8. **messy**   neat   sloppy

9. **corner**   center   edge

10. **curved**   straight   round

11. **polite**   friendly   rude

12. **after**   next   before

◯ = too easy   ▢ = too hard   △ = just right

25

Skill: Clarifying vocabulary

Name _____

Circle the word that means almost the **same** as the word in dark type.

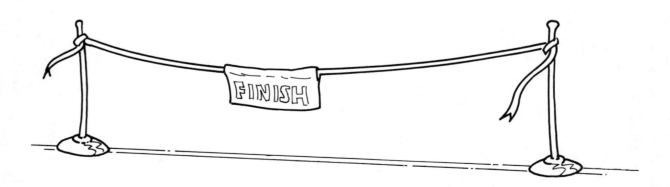

1. **quick**   quiet   speedy

2. **busy**   lazy   active

3. **fat**   chubby   thin

4. **bigger**   best   larger

5. **finest**   good   best

6. **wish**   take   want

7. **kind**   giving   smart

8. **ragged**   torn   used

9. **risky**   dangerous   safe

10. **sign**   signal   ring

11. **limb**   branch   tree

12. **false**   real   fake

◯ = too easy   ▢ = too hard   △ = just right

Skill: Clarifying vocabulary

Name _____

Circle the word that means almost the **same** as the word in dark type.

1. **stingy**   selfish   smelly

2. **angry**   mad   kind

3. **tales**   tails   stories

4. **sob**   weep   grin

5. **eager**   excited   fast

6. **splendid**   good   filthy

7. **motion**   movement   silence

8. **cunning**   clever   quick

9. **stones**   rocks   sand

10. **blanket**   quilt   pillow

11. **share**   give   count

12. **paste**   glue   cut

◯ = too easy   ☐ = too hard   △ = just right

27

Name _____

Draw a picture for each topic. Write one
sentence to tell about your picture.

1. My Best Day

2. My Scariest
Time

3. My Favorite
Things

28

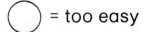
Skill: Relating text to experience

Name ______________________________

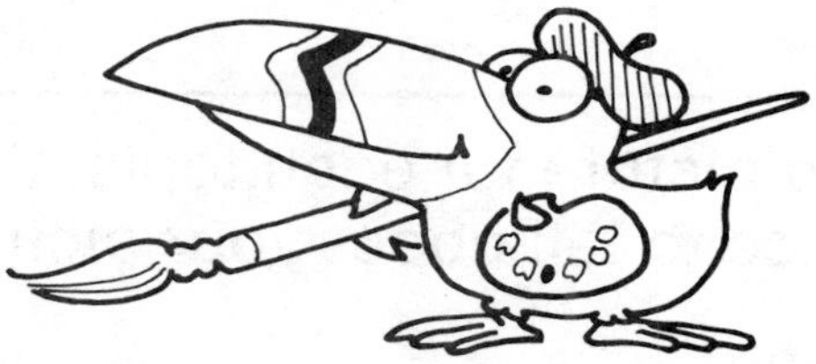

Draw a picture for each topic. Write one sentence to tell about your picture.

1. Seeing the Nurse

____

2. Eating at a Restaurant

____

3. Watching a TV Show

____

○ = too easy   □ = too hard   △ = just right

Skill: Relating text to experience

Name _____

Draw a picture for each topic. Write one sentence to tell about your picture.

1. My Pet

2. My Best Wish

3. My Best Book

○ = too easy   □ = too hard   △ = just right

Skill: Relating text to experience

Name _____

Write three sentences to tell things you
know about each topic.

1. babies _____

   _____

   _____

2. food _____

   _____

   _____

3. books _____

   _____

   _____

4. TV _____

   _____

   _____

5. advertisements _____

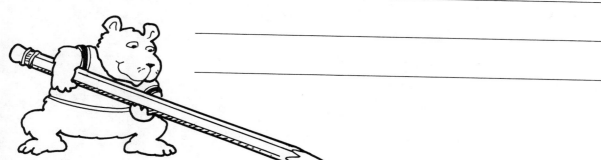

   _____

   _____

◯ = too easy   ▢ = too hard   △ = just right   **31**

Skill: Relating text to experience

Name _____

Write three sentences to tell things you know about each topic.

1. chocolate candy

_____

_____

_____

2. friendly doctors

_____

_____

_____

3. school pictures

_____

_____

_____

4. swimming lessons

_____

_____

_____

5. good manners

_____

_____

_____

32 | ◯ = too easy | ☐ = too hard | △ = just right

Skill: Relating text to experience

Name _____

Write three sentences to tell things you
know about each topic.

1. zoos

_____

_____

_____

2. money

_____

_____

_____

3. newspapers

_____

_____

_____

4. trains

_____

_____

_____

5. flowers

_____

_____

_____

Making Inferences, © 1986 David S. Lake Publishers

◯ = too easy   ▢ = too hard   △ = just right

33

Skill: Relating text to experience

Write three questions you could ask about each book.

Monsters

I. _____
_____
_____
_____
_____

Toys for Girls and Boys

2. _____
_____
_____
_____
_____

Wild Animals

3. _____
_____
_____
_____
_____

34

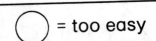 = too easy   ☐ = too hard   △ = just right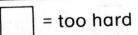

Skill: Relating text to experience

Name _____

Write three questions you could ask about each book.

Funny Jokes

1. _____
_____
_____
_____
_____

Good Food

2. _____
_____
_____
_____
_____

All About Birds

3. _____
_____
_____
_____
_____

◯ = too easy	▢ = too hard	△ = just right

35

Name _____

Draw a picture to show what each
sentence means.

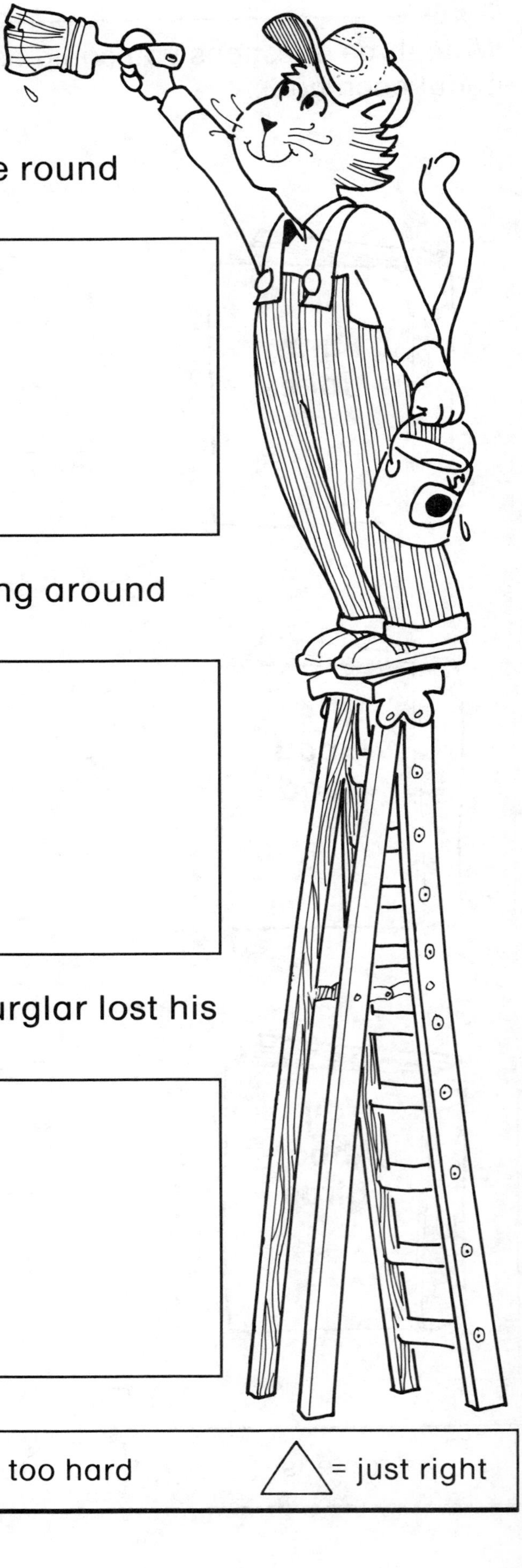

1. I left my yellow lunch box under the round
kitchen table.

2. My teacher wears glasses on a string around
her neck.

3. In the dark of the night, the bald burglar lost his
money.

36

○ = too easy ☐ = too hard △ = just right

Skill: Visualizing

Name _____

Draw a picture to show what each sentence means.

1. The small mean dog chased two boys over the wall and into the pond.

2. Let's make something sweet for your birthday party at the park.

3. The grandmothers' club has five members with many family pictures to share.

○ = too easy   ☐ = too hard   △ = just right

37

Skill: Visualizing

Name _____

Draw a picture to show what each sentence means.

1. The brave old man swam across a river to save his spotted horse.

2. Two frogs sat on a green lily pad and caught flies.

3. The old lady used a bent cane to climb to the top of the snowy mountain.

38

○ = too easy   ☐ = too hard   △ = just right

Skill: Visualizing

Name _____

Draw a picture to show what each part
of the story is about.

1. Once there was a little old man who had a long
beard. He wore a green hat and green shoes.

2. One day the little old man saw a bright rainbow.
He followed the rainbow over a big hill.

3. At the end of the rainbow, he found a green pot
filled with gold. He was very happy.

◯ = too easy   ☐ = too hard   △ = just right

39

Name _____

Draw pictures to show what each part
of the story is about.

1. Two girls and two boys wanted to have a
backward race. They started near the drinking
fountain and ran backward to the brick wall.

2. One girl fell down, one boy bumped into the wall, and the other
two runners missed the wall and ran backward through the gate.

3. Outside the gate was a small pond with a boat nearby. The running
boy fell into the water, and the running girl tripped on the boat.

40

◯ = too easy   ☐ = too hard   △ = just right

Skill: Visualizing

Name _____

Draw pictures to show what each part
of the story is about.

1. Late one night Mrs. Long was walking her big
yellow cat near the rosebushes.

2. Suddenly she saw a huge red monster with three eyes on the end
of its nose and only one large foot.

3. The cat hissed and raised its back. The monster closed its eyes
and hopped away to its spaceship.

◯ = too easy   ▢ = too hard   △ = just right

41

Skill: Visualizing

Name _____

Write what you would do.

1. You are a stray dog and the dogcatcher sees you.

_____

_____

_____

_____

2. You are a rich person in a poor country.

_____

_____

_____

_____

3. You must cook dinner and there is no electricity.

_____

_____

_____

_____

42

◯ = too easy   ▢ = too hard   △ = just right

Skill: Understanding point of view

Name _____

Write what you would do.

1. At your birthday party, you are given three birthday presents that are exactly the same.

_____
_____
_____
_____

2. Your little brother runs away, and you must bring him home.

_____
_____
_____
_____

3. You must make people think you are weak when you are really very strong.

_____
_____
_____
_____

◯ = too easy   ▢ = too hard   △ = just right

43

Skill: Understanding point of view

Name _____

What would you ask the authors? Write your questions below each book title.

I. **Cooking Candy**

_____

_____

2. **Famous Cartoons**

_____

_____

3. **Great Teams in Sports**

_____

_____

4. **All About Cats**

_____

_____

5. **Spiders and More Spiders**

_____

_____

◯ = too easy   ☐ = too hard   △ = just right

Making Inferences © 1986 David S. Lake Publishers

Skill: Understanding point of view

Name _____

Write what you would say.

1. You are a parent and your child is sick.

_____

_____

2. You are a new bike just sold to a child.

_____

_____

3. You are the principal of your school.

_____

_____

4. You are a hammer about to hit a nail.

_____

_____

5. You are an electronic game about to be played.

_____

_____

| ⬤ = too easy | ▢ = too hard | △ = just right | **45** |

Name _____

Write what you would say.

1. You are trying to sell a good toy.

_____

_____

2. You are a teacher with a very good class.

_____

_____

3. You are an apple on a tree.

_____

_____

4. You are a hungry cat who has just found food.

_____

_____

5. You are a fire burning a forest.

_____

_____

46

○ = too easy   □ = too hard   △ = just right

Skill: Understanding point of view

Name _____

Write what you would say.

1. You are the president of your country.

_____

_____

2. You are put in jail by mistake.

_____

_____

3. You are the winner of a large prize.

_____

_____

4. You are sure that you saw a space creature.

_____

_____

5. You are a fish in the ocean.

_____

_____

| ○ = too easy | □ = too hard | △ = just right | **47** |

Skill: Understanding point of view

Name _____

Fill in the blanks to complete each sentence below. Make each sentence tell something different. Then draw pictures to show what each of your sentences means.

1. A duck likes _____   A duck likes _____
   _____

2. _____ live   _____ live
   in the woods.   in the woods.

3. I like to eat _____   I like to eat _____
   _____

48

Skill: Inventing alternatives

Making Inferences, © 1986 David S. Lake Publishers

Name _____

Fill in the blanks to complete each sentence below. Make each sentence tell something different. Then draw pictures to show what each of your sentences means.

1. Mother sat _____

_____

Mother sat _____

_____

2. Let's play _____

Let's play _____

3. I went _____

I went _____

◯ = too easy   ▢ = too hard   △ = just right

49

Making Inferences, © 1986 David S. Lake Publishers

Skill: Inventing alternatives

Fill in the blanks to complete each sentence below. Make each sentence tell something different. Then draw pictures to show what each of your sentences means.

1. _____ are

animals with _____

2. _____ likes

to _____

3. My _____ is

filled with _____

1. _____ are

animals with _____

2. _____ likes

to _____

3. My _____ is

filled with _____

50

◯ = too easy   ▢ = too hard   △ = just right

Skill: Inventing alternatives

Making Inferences, © 1986 David S. Lake Publishers

Making Inferences, © 1986 David S. Lake Publishers

Name _____

Draw a picture to show what each
sentence means. Then write three more
sentences to tell what happened next.

1. Little Red Riding Hood was late for school.

2. Cinderella's glass slipper fit the wicked
   stepmother.

◯ = too easy   ☐ = too hard   △ = just right

51

Name _____

Draw a picture to show what each
sentence means. Then write three more
sentences to tell what happened next.

1. The small cars and trucks were driven by cats
   and dogs.

```
┌─────────────────────────────────────────┐
│                                           │
│                                           │
│                                           │
│                                           │
│                                           │
└─────────────────────────────────────────┘
```

_____

_____

_____

2. They looked out the window and saw a giraffe
   in the street.

```
┌─────────────────────────────────────────┐
│                                           │
│                                           │
│                                           │
│                                           │
│                                           │
└─────────────────────────────────────────┘
```

_____

_____

_____

52

○ = too easy   □ = too hard   △ = just right

Name _____

Draw a picture to show what each sentence means. Then write three more sentences to tell what happened next.

1. Elephants can fly, and they eat only bananas.

2. The trees in the park are made of chocolate.

Name _____

Draw a picture to show what will happen next. Then write a sentence to tell about your picture.

1. You drop a very good dish when no one is at home.

2. You find a wallet on the street, and you take it to the police.

3. Your parents take you to a fancy restaurant.

54 | ◯ = too easy | ▢ = too hard | △ = just right

Skill: Predicting consequences and conclusions

Name _____

Draw a picture to show what will happen next. Then write a sentence to tell about your picture.

1. A big dog is trying to take your lunch.

_____
_____

2. You and your friends are playing in the park when it begins to rain.

_____
_____

3. Your good friend just gave you a present that you do not want.

_____
_____

○ = too easy   □ = too hard   △ = just right

55

Name _____

Draw a picture to show what will happen next. Then write a sentence to tell about your picture.

1. You are riding the bus and you miss the place you should have gotten off.

_____

2. Every day you brush your teeth carefully. You do not eat sweets. Now you go to see the dentist.

_____

3. Your neighbor gives you a new bike.

_____

56

◯ = too easy   ▢ = too hard   △ = just right

Skill: Predicting consequences and conclusions

Making Inferences, © 1986 David S. Lake Publishers

Name _____

Draw a picture to show what will happen next. Then write a sentence to tell about your picture.

1. You are in a costume parade.

2. The eye doctor says you need glasses.

3. You just found ten dollars.

⬭ = too easy   ▭ = too hard   △ = just right

57

Making Inferences, © 1986 David S. Lake Publishers

Skill: Predicting consequences and conclusions

Name _____

Draw a picture to show what will happen next. Then write a sentence to tell about your picture.

1. You buy an ice-cream cone, and it falls on the sidewalk before you take a bite.

_____
_____

2. You get a bunny for a pet.

_____
_____

3. Your family has a surprise party for you, and you are very surprised.

_____
_____

58

◯ = too easy   ▢ = too hard   △ = just right

Skill: Predicting consequences and conclusions

Answer Key

Page 7
Accept appropriate pictures.

Page 8
Accept appropriate pictures.

Page 9
Accept appropriate pictures.

Page 10
Accept appropriate pictures.

Page 11
Accept appropriate events in sequence.

Page 12
Accept appropriate events in sequence.

Page 13
The following words should be written on the lines (accept reasonable variations): 1. There was a big snowfall, 2. we looked for wood, 3. Once we made ice cream, 4. Sue went to a party, 5. We mixed sugar and butter, 6. she married the prince.

Page 14
The following words should be written on the lines (accept reasonable variations): 1. he cried, 2. Finally she got a dog, 3. my birthday arrived, 4. Then we mixed the batter, 5. We went inside, 6. Finally he opened the present.

Page 15
Accept appropriate adjectives.

Page 16
Accept appropriate adjectives.

Page 17
Accept appropriate responses which indicate *how*.

Page 18
Accept appropriate pictures and responses.

Page 19
Accept appropriate pictures and responses.

Page 20
Accept appropriate pictures and responses.

Page 21
Accept appropriate responses (unusual comparisons possible).

Page 22
Accept appropriate responses.

Page 23
Accept appropriate responses.

Page 24
The following words should be circled:
1. gloomy, 2. pretty, 3. sad, 4. stupid,
5. seek, 6. sink, 7. destroy, 8. open,
9. harden, 10. few, 11. worst, 12. lose.

Page 25
The following words should be circled:
1. future, 2. never, 3. well, 4. spend,
5. under, 6. midnight, 7. take, 8. neat,
9. center, 10. straight, 11. rude, 12. before.

Page 26
The following words should be circled:
1. speedy, 2. active, 3. chubby, 4. larger,
5. best, 6. want, 7. giving, 8. torn,
9. dangerous, 10. signal, 11. branch,
12. fake.

Page 27
The following words should be circled:
1. selfish, 2. mad, 3. stories, 4. weep,
5. excited, 6. good, 7. movement, 8. clever,
9. rocks, 10. quilt, 11. give, 12. glue.

Page 28
Accept appropriate pictures and responses.

Page 29
Accept appropriate pictures and responses.

Page 30
Accept appropriate pictures and responses.

Page 31
Accept appropriate responses.

Page 32
Accept appropriate responses.

Page 33
Accept appropriate responses.

Page 34
Accept appropriate questions.

Page 35
Accept appropriate questions.

Page 36
Accept appropriate pictures.

Page 37
Accept appropriate pictures.

Page 38
Accept appropriate pictures.

Page 39
Accept appropriate pictures.

Page 40
Accept appropriate pictures.

Page 41
Accept appropriate pictures.

Page 42
Accept appropriate responses.

Page 43
Accept appropriate responses.

Page 44
Accept appropriate questions.

Page 45
Accept appropriate responses.

Page 46
Accept appropriate responses.

Page 47
Accept appropriate responses.

Page 48
Accept appropriate pictures and responses.

Page 49
Accept appropriate pictures and responses.

Page 50
Accept appropriate pictures and responses.

Page 51

Accept appropriate pictures and responses.

Page 52

Accept appropriate pictures and responses.

Page 53

Accept appropriate pictures and responses.

Page 54

Accept appropriate pictures and responses.

Page 55

Accept appropriate pictures and responses.

Page 56

Accept appropriate pictures and responses.

Page 57

Accept appropriate pictures and responses.

Page 58

Accept appropriate pictures and responses.

Intent on Inferences

Grades 4–6

Contents

Introduction

The lessons in this workbook develop eight subskills for making inferences. The reproducible worksheets are organized into sections, each section pertaining to one of the eight subskills:

1. **Finding Sequence Clues**
2. **Using Descriptive Language**
3. **Clarifying Vocabulary**
4. **Relating Text to Experience**
5. **Visualizing**
6. **Understanding Point of View**
7. **Inventing Alternatives**
8. **Predicting Consequences and Conclusions**

At the conclusion of each activity is an evaluation code box.

An evaluation of item difficulty can be made by enclosing the item number within one of the shapes shown in the box to relay the coded message. Another way to use the code box is simply to shade in the shape that best evaluates the page. This evaluation might be made by the teacher, the student,

a tutor, or a team. The code is designed to help determine skill areas needing further attention.

The following section suggests additional activities for continued practice in making inferences.

Additional Activities

1. Functional Comprehension
Familiarize students with the world of words in everyday life. Present vocabulary through the exploration of checkbooks, charge cards, coupons, measurements, catalogs, forms, game directions, menus, public notices, brochures, packaging print, maps, and other printed matter. Discuss the types of print and the phrasings used. Note how writing is used to influence us, inform us, and help us live better.

2. Personification
Have students imagine that they can get into another skin. Have them take a different viewpoint, and write or talk about it. For example, ask, "How would you feel if you were the wolf in 'Little Red Riding Hood'?"

3. Polar Opposites

Have students discuss and evaluate characters by measuring their qualities on a numeric scale. For example: Goldilocks is

_____ .

brave ____ ____ ____ ____ ____ scared
       5   4   3   2   1

4. Key Words

Use cloze activities for reading and writing. Discuss how a variety of responses may be accepted for some answers. For example: Mary _____ and stayed home from school.

5. Perception

Use mazes, optical illusions, puzzles, and interesting pictures to get students to look at things in several ways. Be sure to discuss different viewpoints and accept varying logical responses.

6. Interview

Ask three questions of any imaginary person (for example, a lottery winner, an ambulance attendant). Discuss the possible responses from the imaginary person.

7. Deep Processing

Focus on text material. Use such methods as outlining, summarizing, note-taking, visualizing, elaborating, reporting, illustrating, and diagramming.

8. Book Reports

Use a variety of vehicles for sharing readers' responses to stories or books. Mobiles, graphs, diaries, place mats, postcards, letters, surveys, questionnaires, discussion panels, pantomimes, debates, collections, puzzles, dioramas, scrapbooks, and interviews may be used to summarize and clarify reading experiences.

9. Figurative Language

Use metaphors and similes to describe characters and events in a story. For example: Long John Silver, in *Treasure Island,* is as scary as _____ .

10. Questioning

Have the readers ask questions before, during, and after reading. Include questions having multiple correct responses. Help readers identify individual purposes for reading and questioning.

Name _____

Underline the word or words in each
sentence that tell **when.**

1. Some of our friends met at the library after school.

2. We always bring new books for the children.

3. Who discovered America before Columbus arrived in 1492?

4. She takes a piano lesson every Wednesday.

5. Let's go to the museum; then we will write our report at home.

6. The building lost electricity during the storm.

7. Troublemakers are found in school once in a while.

8. Famous writers will visit our class in a few months.

9. Next I want to congratulate the second-place winners.

10. Did you eat a hearty breakfast this morning?

11. When summer comes, vacation season begins.

12. The meeting will begin when everyone arrives.

8 | ◯ = too easy | ▢ = too hard | △ = just right |

Skill: Finding sequence clues

Intent on Inferences, © 1986 David S. Lake Publishers

Name _____

Underline the words in each sentence that tell **when.**

1. Jennifer baked another cake as soon as the first cake was eaten.

2. The teacher smiled as she graded the reports.

3. A parade of exotic animals will be coming to town soon.

4. During our practice, the troublesome child interrupted us.

5. At last the long journey was ended!

6. By the next summer, the trees had grown taller.

7. Every now and then, we shop at a different market.

8. Long ago, people lived in small villages.

9. Early the next morning, we completed the assignment.

10. Electric appliances were not used hundreds of years ago.

11. In the winter, we will go skating on the pond.

12. By the end of the day, he was tired from work.

Intent on Inferences, © 1986 David S. Lake Publishers

◯ = too easy   ▢ = too hard   △ = just right

7

Skill: Finding sequence clues

Name _____

Read each sentence. Then write the event that happened **first**.

1. After we traveled a long way, we came to a small city.

   _____

2. Before we gave the concert, we practiced for many hours.

   _____

3. We went to the play as soon as we were dressed.

   _____

4. James bought the ingredients yesterday for the cookies that he baked

   today. _____

5. Last month the class made a model city that won an award in yesterday's

   competition. _____

6. After the long cold winter, the people were grateful for the warm spring

   weather. _____

7. Some children learn to read before they enter school.

   _____

8. John needed braces. Subsequently, the doctor prescribed them.

   _____

9. Glenda enjoyed school. Later she worked as a teacher.

   _____

10. The best team won the game and celebrated afterward.

    _____

| ◯ = too easy | ▢ = too hard | △ = just right | **9** |

Name _____

Read each sentence. Then write the event
that happened **second**.

1. After several hours of waiting in line, Janice bought her tickets.

   _____

2. We learned to draw well after taking art lessons.

   _____

3. Amanda finally opened the package that had arrived last week.

   _____

4. Previously, the vacationing family had not found a place to stay, so they
   were lucky to find a motel last night.

   _____

5. Jim got into trouble by trying to get out of work.

   _____

6. Dick is happy because he was elected vice president.

   _____

7. The fire fighters did not talk before the blaze was out.

   _____

8. Harry's doctor advised him to drink water. Now he drinks water three
   times a day. _____

9. During the night it was raining, but the sky cleared by morning.

   _____

10. We walked along the beach. Later we picnicked near the monument.

   _____

10 | ◯ = too easy | ▢ = too hard | △ = just right

Skill: Finding sequence clues

Name _____

Use the sequence clues to write a story for each topic below.

1. **carving a turkey**

   First _____

   Next _____

   Then _____

   At last _____

2. **planning a party**

   First _____

   Next _____

   Then _____

   At last _____

3. **daydreaming**

   First _____

   Next _____

   Then _____

   Finally _____

4. **traveling**

   First _____

   Next _____

   Then _____

   Finally _____

◯ = too easy	▢ = too hard	△ = just right

11

Skill: Finding sequence clues

Name _____

Use the sequence clues to write a story for each topic below.

1. **making breakfast**

   Long ago _____

   Later _____

   Now _____

   In the future _____

2. **working at home**

   Last week _____

   Today _____

   Tomorrow _____

   Next week _____

3. **going to school**

   Yesterday _____

   In a few months _____

   Next year _____

   In the near future _____

4. **helping friends**

   Once _____

   Now _____

   During _____

   Next _____

12

◯ = too easy   ▢ = too hard   △ = just right

Skill: Finding sequence clues

Name _____

Write four words to describe each topic below.

1. a new car

_____

_____

_____

_____

2. a broken leg

_____

_____

_____

_____

3. your home

_____

_____

_____

_____

4. a gift

_____

_____

_____

_____

5. a pizza

_____

_____

_____

_____

6. a good meal

_____

_____

_____

_____

7. a headache

_____

_____

_____

_____

8. a television show

_____

_____

_____

_____

9. a teacher

_____

_____

_____

_____

10. a movie

_____

_____

_____

_____

⃝ = too easy   ▢ = too hard   △ = just right

13

Skill: Using descriptive language

Name _____

Write four words to describe each topic below.

1. those people

_____
_____
_____
_____

2. your clothes

_____
_____
_____
_____

3. this watch

_____
_____
_____
_____

4. a game

_____
_____
_____
_____

5. their house

_____
_____
_____
_____

6. four animals

_____
_____
_____
_____

7. that bus

_____
_____
_____
_____

8. this computer

_____
_____
_____
_____

9. a story

_____
_____
_____
_____

10. a tree

_____
_____
_____
_____

14 ⃝ = too easy   ☐ = too hard   △ = just right

Skill: Using descriptive language

Name _____

Write four words to describe each topic below.

1. parties

_____
_____
_____
_____

2. friends

_____
_____
_____
_____

3. happiness

_____
_____
_____
_____

4. exercise

_____
_____
_____
_____

5. music

_____
_____
_____
_____

6. poetry

_____
_____
_____
_____

7. travel

_____
_____
_____
_____

8. wilderness

_____
_____
_____
_____

9. trains

_____
_____
_____
_____

10. birds

_____
_____
_____
_____

○ = too easy   ☐ = too hard   △ = just right

15

Intent on Inferences, © 1986 David S. Lake Publishers

Skill: Using descriptive language

Name _____

Write four words to describe each activity below.

1. running

_____
_____
_____
_____

2. writing

_____
_____
_____
_____

3. growing

_____
_____
_____
_____

4. losing

_____
_____
_____
_____

5. driving

_____
_____
_____
_____

6. eating

_____
_____
_____
_____

7. shopping

_____
_____
_____
_____

8. learning

_____
_____
_____
_____

9. thinking

_____
_____
_____
_____

10. reading

_____
_____
_____
_____

16

◯ = too easy   ▢ = too hard   △ = just right

Skill: Using descriptive language

Name _____

Fill in the blanks to complete each sentence.

1. I am as big as _____ .

2. Don't dance like _____ .

3. The weather is as disagreeable as _____ .

4. The whole class worked like _____ .

5. The man was as tall as _____ .

6. Let's climb as high as _____ .

7. He sang the song like _____ .

8. Try to be as quiet as _____ .

9. Fast runners look like _____ .

10. Please eat like _____ .

11. My hair looks like _____ .

12. Her teeth seem white as _____ .

◯ = too easy   ☐ = too hard   △ = just right   **17**

Skill: Using descriptive language

Name _____

Fill in the blanks to describe **how.**

1. My dad sings a song _____ .

2. I always eat breakfast _____ .

3. Let's _____ tour the zoo.

4. Little children _____ learn new things.

5. Please finish your homework _____ .

6. I _____ rode the bicycle before it broke.

7. My sister _____ fixed the machine.

8. During class Pat painted _____ .

9. After school we met our friends _____ .

10. Next summer we will go skydiving _____ .

11. Mix the vegetables together _____ .

12. Don't pack his clothes _____ .

18

Skill: Using descriptive language

Name _____

Read the incomplete story below. Fill in the blanks so the story makes sense. Use a different word in each blank.

At first there was only one _____ , _____ monkey.

It had _____ _____ teeth and a _____ ,

_____ tail. Then _____

_____ monkeys arrived. The new animals ran _____

to the first monkey. All of the monkeys played _____ on the

swings. All at once the _____ _____ monkey moved

_____ away from the others. He _____ picked up his

_____ _____ dish and threw it _____ at

the _____ monkey! In the end, all _____

_____ monkeys were _____ put in _____

_____ cage.

○ = too easy   □ = too hard   △ = just right

19

Skill: Using descriptive language

Name _____

Read the incomplete story below. Fill in the blanks so the story makes sense. Use a different word in each blank.

Once upon a time, there was a _____ , _____

man. He wore _____ , _____ clothes and

a _____ hat. This _____ man liked to sell

_____ _____ things to the _____

_____ people. One day the _____ people discovered

that there was something _____ about the _____

things the _____ man was selling. So they gave him some

_____ things to sell. Now the _____ ,

_____ man sells _____ , _____ things

to the people.

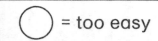

20 ◯ = too easy   ▢ = too hard   △ = just right

Skill: Using descriptive language

Name _____

For each exercise, circle the word that means
the **opposite** of the word in dark type. Use a
dictionary if you need help.

1. **awkward**   clumsy   adept
2. **opponent**   teammate   enemy
3. **ridiculous**   admirable   excellent
4. **worship**   despise   adore
5. **profit**   lose   succeed
6. **flexible**   fancy   rigid
7. **affection**   indifference love
8. **fearless**   strong   scared
9. **preceding**   following   giving
10. **alert**   dangerous   inattentive
11. **retain**   review   discard
12. **ready**   unprepared   begin
13. **frequent**   rare   enjoyable
14. **expand**   contract   enlarge
15. **income**   exit   expense
16. **courage**   cowardice   bravery
17. **cheap**   inexpensive   costly
18. **decay**   flourish   rot
19. **undecided**   convinced   concluded
20. **shallow**   deep   wet

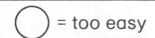 = too easy    = too hard   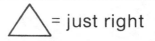 = just right

21

Skill: Clarifying vocabulary

Name _____

For each word below, write a word that means the **opposite.** Use a dictionary if you need help.

1. admire _____

2. power _____

3. destroy _____

4. absent _____

5. beneath _____

6. near _____

7. equal _____

8. agony _____

9. break _____

10. gloomy _____

11. vacant _____

12. doubtful _____

13. grand _____

14. smooth _____

15. shrewd _____

16. shade _____

17. active _____

18. overlook _____

19. vanish _____

20. deliver _____

21. swift _____

22. together _____

23. wild _____

24. weaken _____

22

◯ = too easy   ▢ = too hard   △ = just right

Skill: Clarifying vocabulary

Name _____

Circle the word that means almost the **same** as the word in dark type. Use a dictionary if you need help.

1. **mend**   repair   spoil

2. **standard**   rule   surprise

3. **vain**   modest   conceited

4. **obey**   confuse   comply

5. **neglect**   respect   ignore

6. **neat**   tidy   famous

7. **noisy**   loud   quiet

8. **retain**   keep   discard

9. **stern**   easygoing   harsh

10. **usual**   regular   odd

11. **resolve**   decide   respond

12. **choice**   charity   option

13. **quick**   detached   swift

14. **aware**   conscious   dead

15. **bashful**   modest   shy

16. **disturb**   annoy   assist

17. **liberty**   magazine   freedom

18. **cherish**   love   explain

19. **spoil**   corrupt   use

20. **mingle**   avoid   blend

◯ = too easy   ▢ = too hard   △ = just right

23

Skill: Clarifying vocabulary

Name _____

For each word below, write a word that means almost the **same**. Use a dictionary if you need help.

1. clever _____

2. zest _____

3. humor _____

4. incorrect _____

5. price _____

6. conquer _____

7. strange _____

8. injure _____

9. hazy _____

10. speedy _____

11. hideous _____

12. assist _____

13. moist _____

14. chuckle _____

15. cheat _____

16. astonish _____

17. assault _____

18. anger _____

19. reply _____

20. trouble _____

21. friend _____

22. timid _____

23. sharp _____

24. increase _____

24 ◯ = too easy ☐ = too hard △ = just right

Skill: Clarifying vocabulary

Name _____

Complete the word groups by writing one
related word in each space.

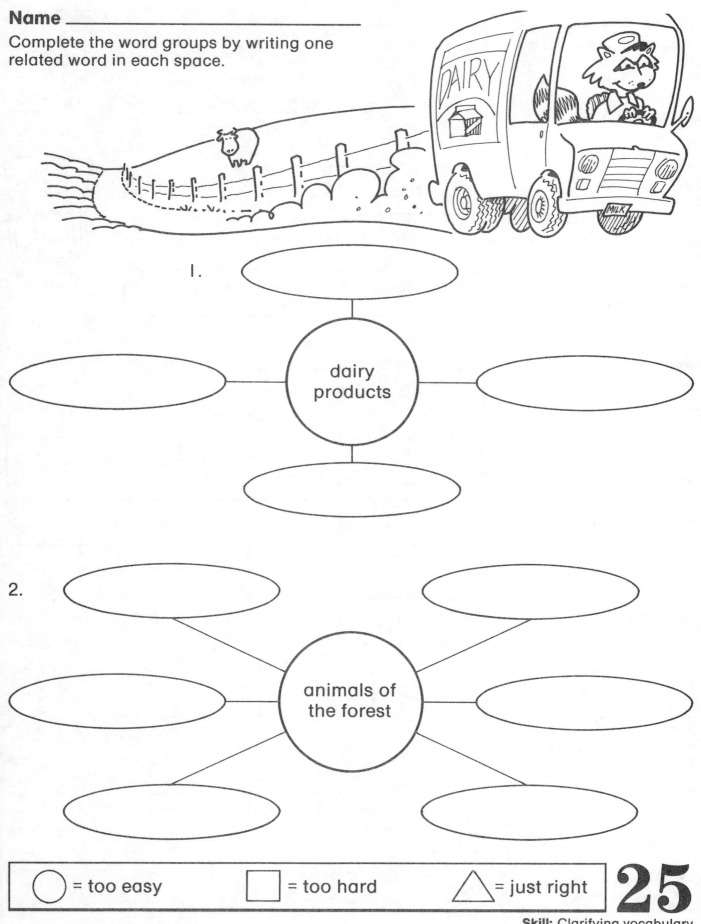

I.

dairy
products

2.

animals of
the forest

◯ = too easy   ▢ = too hard   △ = just right

25

Skill: Clarifying vocabulary

Name _____

Complete the word groups by writing one or
more related words in each box.

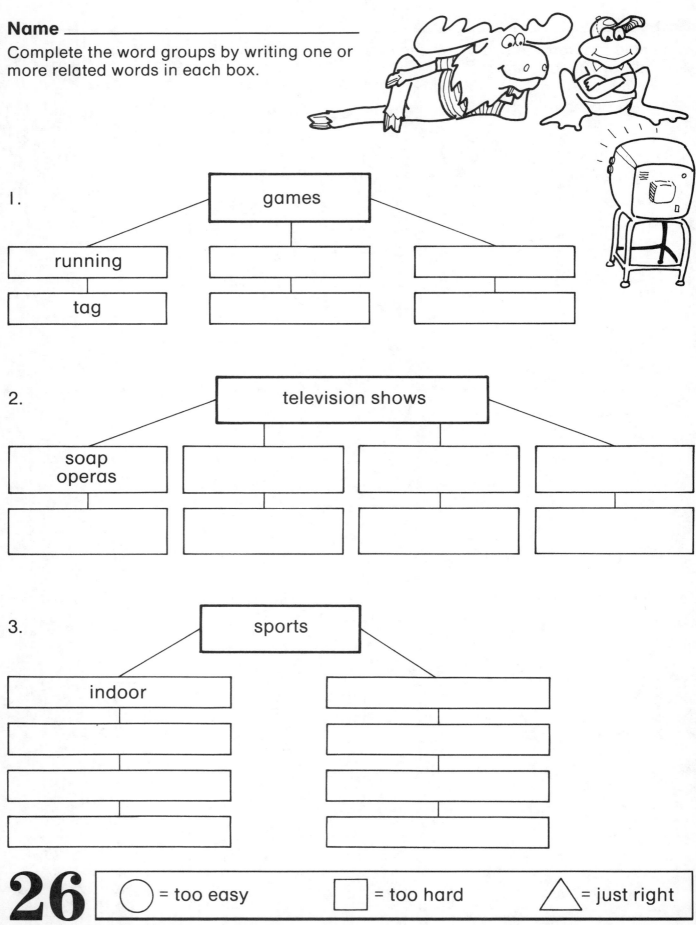

1.

games

running		

tag		

2.

television shows

soap operas			

3.

sports

indoor	

○ = too easy   □ = too hard   △ = just right

Skill: Clarifying vocabulary

Name _____

Write one or two sentences to describe each experience.

1. your earliest memory _____
   _____

2. your worst punishment _____
   _____

3. your best vacation _____
   _____

4. your worst moment _____
   _____

5. your best birthday _____
   _____

6. your biggest fear _____
   _____

7. your last dental appointment _____
   _____

8. your most recent purchase _____
   _____

⬤ = too easy   ▢ = too hard   △ = just right

27

Name _____

Write one or two sentences to describe each experience.

1. your most recent dream _____

_____

2. your most embarrassing moment _____

_____

3. your most treasured gift _____

_____

4. your latest responsibility _____

_____

5. your favorite family activity _____

_____

6. your bravest act _____

_____

7. your most recent regret _____

_____

8. your latest hope _____

_____

28 ◯ = too easy ☐ = too hard △ = just right

Skill: Relating text to experience

Name ______________________

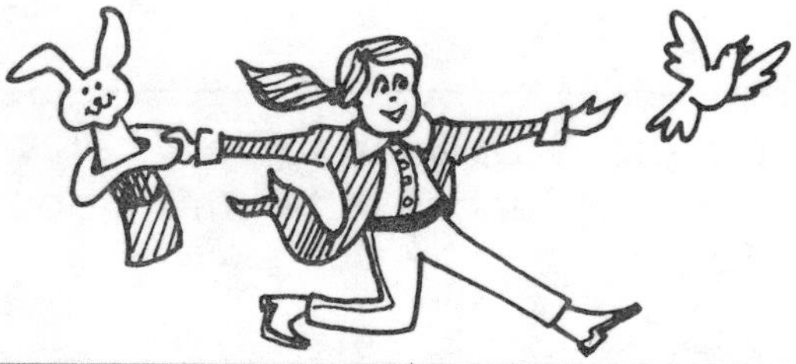

Draw a picture for each topic. Then write one or two sentences to tell more about your picture.

1. a new invention

____

____

2. a kind of magic

____

____

3. an imaginary person

____

____

○ = too easy □ = too hard △ = just right

Skill: Relating text to experience

Name _____

Draw a picture for each topic. Then write one or two sentences to tell more about your picture.

1. telephoning your friend

_____

_____

2. eating at a restaurant

_____

_____

3. traveling on vacation

_____

_____

30 ⬭ = too easy   ◻ = too hard   △ = just right

Skill: Relating text to experience

Name ______________________________

Draw a picture for each topic. Then write one or two sentences to tell more about your picture.

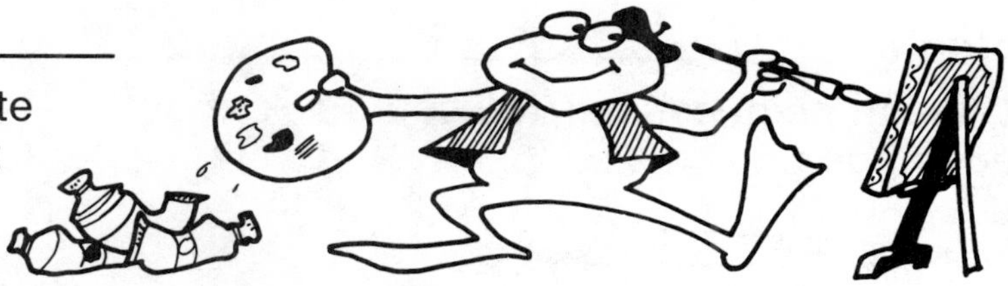

1. a visit to the dentist

____

____

2. a famous landmark

____

____

3. a ride in an amusement park

____

____

○ = too easy   □ = too hard   △ = just right

Skill: Relating text to experience

Name _____

Write three questions you could ask about each book.

Insects for Food!

1. _____
_____
_____
_____
_____

Adult School

2. _____
_____
_____
_____
_____
_____

Hypnotism

3. _____
_____
_____
_____
_____

Bigfoot

4. _____
_____
_____
_____
_____

32   ◯ = too easy   ▢ = too hard   △ = just right

Skill: Relating text to experience

Name _____

Write three sentences that tell things you
know about each topic.

1. adults _____
_____
_____

2. wealth _____
_____
_____

3. sickness _____
_____
_____

4. clubs _____
_____
_____

5. travel _____
_____
_____

6. sports _____
_____
_____

7. plants _____
_____
_____

8. foreign languages _____
_____
_____

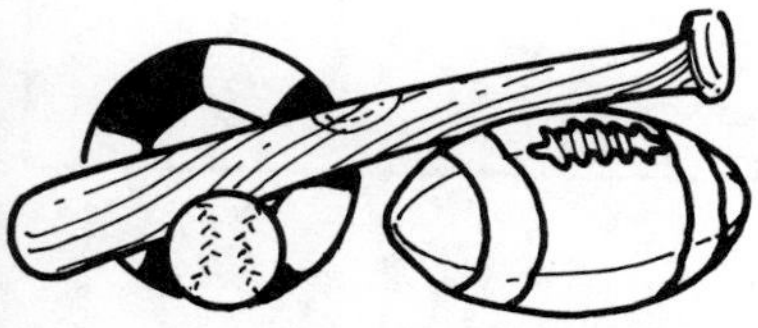

◯ = too easy   ☐ = too hard   △ = just right

33

Skill: Relating text to experience

Name _____

Draw a picture to show what each sentence means.

1. More than one prisoner has attempted to escape from this water-surrounded, rock-covered prison.

2. A screaming infant was carried past the tempting articles on the toy-store shelves and was deposited safely in protective arms.

3. The magnificent feast ended abruptly when an obese waiter dropped the gooey desert.

34

◯ = too easy   ▢ = too hard   △ = just right

Skill: Visualizing

Name _____

Draw a picture to show what each sentence means.

1. The driver of the battered pickup truck delivered six hens to the wrong store.

2. Several hairy gorillas lived on the tree-covered island.

3. The ancient gentlemen hastened to an outdoor feast.

○ = too easy   ☐ = too hard   △ = just right

35

Name _____

Draw a picture to show what each sentence means.

1. A howling wind swept around the forest cabin and encouraged the hikers to pull fur hats over their heads.

2. I dropped my new glasses into the lake and watched from a boat as the giant fish consumed them.

3. Six dancing flamingos joined four grinning baboons for the fireworks.

36

◯ = too easy   ☐ = too hard   △ = just right

Skill: Visualizing

Name _____

Fill in the blanks to complete the story. Then
draw pictures to illustrate each part of your story.

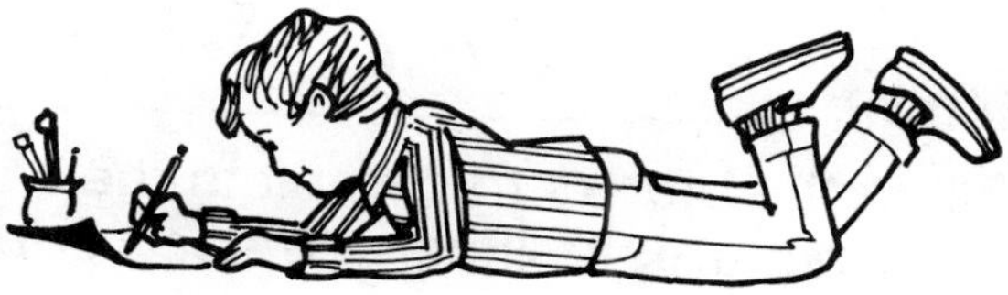

1. Once upon a time, there was a _____

_____

2. The _____ could not _____

_____

3. After a long vacation, _____

_____

⬭ = too easy   ▢ = too hard   △ = just right

37

Skill: Visualizing

Name _____

Fill in the blanks to complete the story. Then
draw pictures to illustrate each part of your story.

1. One problem at our school _____

_____

_____

2. To solve the problem, _____

_____

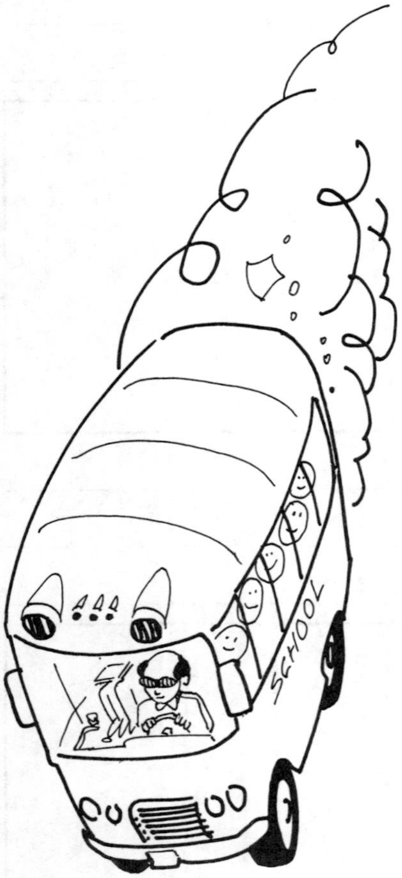

3. Finally _____

_____

38

Skill: Visualizing

◯ = too easy   ▢ = too hard   △ = just right

Name _____

Fill in the blanks to complete the story. Then draw pictures to illustrate each part of your story.

1. A very new invention is the _____

_____

_____

2. This contraption can _____

_____

_____

3. I would like to use this invention _____

_____

_____

◯ = too easy   ☐ = too hard   △ = just right

39

Skill: Visualizing

Name _____

Write what you would say.

1. You are trying to sell your friends a new racing bike.

_____
_____
_____

2. You are the leader of a country that is surrendering after losing a war.

_____
_____
_____

3. You are a priceless vase in the hands of a clumsy child.

_____
_____
_____

4. You are a cave dweller who has just discovered fire.

_____
_____
_____

5. You are the principal of your own school.

_____
_____
_____

40

◯ = too easy   ▢ = too hard   △ = just right

Name _____

Write what you would say.

1. You are asked to describe your favorite food to a Martian.

   _____
   _____
   _____

2. You are an electronic game in the hands of an expert player.

   _____
   _____
   _____

3. You are sure you have just seen an unidentified flying object (UFO).

   _____
   _____
   _____

4. You are a great white shark.

   _____
   _____
   _____

5. You have just won one million dollars in the lottery.

   _____
   _____
   _____

◯ = too easy   ▢ = too hard   △ = just right

41

Skill: Understanding point of view

Name _____

What would you ask the authors? Write your questions below each book title.

1. **Cooking Diet Desserts**

_____

_____

_____

2. **The Ten Most Popular Television Shows**

_____

_____

_____

3. **Great Teams in Sports**

_____

_____

_____

4. **Making Commercials**

_____

_____

_____

5. **Adventures in Space**

_____

_____

_____

◯ = too easy   ▢ = too hard   △ = just right

Skill: Understanding point of view

Name _____

What would you ask the authors? Write your questions below each book title.

1. **The Super Picture Dictionary**

_____
_____
_____

2. **Historic Flags**

_____
_____
_____

3. **Modern Cartoons**

_____
_____
_____
_____

4. **The Unending Mystery**

_____
_____
_____

5. **Super Spy Adventures**

_____
_____
_____
_____

◯ = too easy   ▢ = too hard   △ = just right

43

Name _____

Write what you would do.

1. You are preparing dinner for your class, and the electricity goes off.

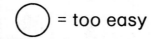

_____
_____
_____

2. You are traveling in a foreign country, and you cannot speak the language.

_____
_____
_____

3. Your best friend is wrongly accused of shoplifting.

_____
_____
_____

4. Your best friend is correctly accused of shoplifting.

_____
_____
_____

5. You are the wealthy ruler of a poor country.

_____
_____
_____

44

Skill: Understanding point of view

Name _____

Write what you would do.

1. You must make people believe you are strong when you are really weak.

   _____
   _____
   _____

2. Your parents are kidnapped and held for ransom.

   _____
   _____
   _____

3. Your new job requires that you leave the country for two years.

   _____
   _____
   _____

4. You are trying to teach a young child to read.

   _____
   _____
   _____

5. It is opening night, and your costar is sick.

   _____
   _____
   _____

○ = too easy   ☐ = too hard   △ = just right

45

Skill: Understanding point of view

Name _____

Fill in the blanks to complete each sentence below. Make each sentence tell something different. Then draw pictures to show what each of your sentences means.

1. Young children enjoy _____

_____

_____

Young children enjoy _____

_____

_____

2. Animals in the forest _____

_____

Animals in the forest _____

_____

3. I enjoy _____

_____

_____

I enjoy _____

_____

_____

46

◯ = too easy   ▢ = too hard   △ = just right

Skill: Inventing alternatives

Name _____

Fill in the blanks to complete each sentence below. Make each sentence tell something different. Then draw pictures to show what your sentences mean.

1. The woman _____

_____

_____

The woman _____

_____

_____

2. Let's write a _____

for the _____

_____

Let's write a _____

for the _____

3. The _____

traveled in a _____

_____

The _____

traveled in a _____

Name _____

Fill in the blanks to complete each sentence below. Make each sentence tell something different. Then draw pictures to show what your sentences mean.

1. _____ are

animals with _____

_____

_____ are

animals with _____

_____

2. _____ likes to

_____

_____ likes to

_____

3. My _____ is

fitted with _____

_____

My _____ is

fitted with _____

_____

◯ = too easy   ▢ = too hard   △ = just right

Skill: Inventing alternatives

Name _____

Draw pictures to show what the sentences mean. Then write three more sentences to tell what could happen next.

1. The surface of the planet was made of bubble gum! We were also surprised by the inhabitants of the planet.

_____

_____

_____

2. During the night the trees in the forest moved from one place to another.

_____

_____

_____

◯ = too easy   ▢ = too hard   △ = just right

49

Name _____

Draw a picture to show what each sentence means. Then write three more sentences to tell what could happen next.

1. Several trucks made of high-bounce rubber collided on the Rainbow Bridge.

_____

_____

_____

2. With extra equipment the swimmers stayed underwater and completed their work.

_____

_____

_____

50 ◯ = too easy ▢ = too hard △ = just right

Name _____

Tell how each story might have ended. Write three or four sentences to explain what would happen next.

1. Sleeping Beauty did not want to marry the prince.

_____
_____
_____
_____

2. Cinderella's fairy godmother was captured by the stepmother.

_____
_____
_____
_____

3. Everyone on Earth looked exactly alike.

_____
_____
_____
_____

◯ = too easy   ☐ = too hard   △ = just right

51

Name _____

Write three or four sentences to explain what will happen next.

1. Your plane, destined for New York, is hijacked to Paris.

_____

_____

_____

_____

2. You exercise regularly, eat only healthful foods, and sleep eight hours nightly. Now you must visit your doctor for a complete physical.

_____

_____

_____

_____

3. A person is trying to sell you a vacuum cleaner you do not want, but you are very interested in the bonus prize you are offered if you buy the vacuum cleaner.

_____

_____

_____

_____

52

◯ = too easy ☐ = too hard △ = just right

Skill: Predicting consequences and conclusions

Name _____

Write three or four sentences to explain
what will happen next.

1. You drop a precious bowl when no one
   else is around.

   _____

   _____

   _____

   _____

2. You find a purse on the street. Next you flag a
   police officer.

   _____

   _____

   _____

   _____

3. You are the guest of a famous movie star for dinner
   at a fancy restaurant.

   _____

   _____

   _____

   _____

54 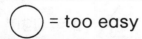 = too easy ☐ = too hard △ = just right

Skill: Predicting consequences and conclusions

Intent on Inferences, © 1986 David S. Lake Publishers

Name _____

Write three or four sentences to explain
what will happen next.

1. You are invited to be sawed in half by a magician.

   _____

   _____

   _____

   _____

   _____

2. Two hundred kindergarten children plan to have a
   costume parade.

   _____

   _____

   _____

   _____

   _____

3. The books you need for an important test are
   locked in your classroom.

   _____

   _____

   _____

   _____

   _____

◯ = too easy   ▢ = too hard   △ = just right

53

Skill: Predicting consequences and conclusions

Name _____

Write three or four sentences to explain
what will happen next.

1. A giant gorilla is admiring your lunch.

_____

_____

_____

_____

_____

2. Your good friend just gave you a present that you
do not want.

_____

_____

_____

_____

_____

3. You are sailing in shark-infested water when
lightning strikes your boat.

_____

_____

_____

_____

_____

◯ = too easy   ☐ = too hard   △ = just right

55

Skill: Predicting consequences and conclusions

Name _____

Write three or four sentences to explain
what will happen next.

1. You have just arrived at summer camp. As your
   family drives away, you discover they still have
   your clothes and sleeping bag in the car.

   _____
   _____
   _____
   _____
   _____

2. Your friend wins a trip to Alaska and invites
   you along.

   _____
   _____
   _____
   _____
   _____

3. At summer camp, someone pours syrup in your
   hair while you are sleeping.

   _____
   _____
   _____
   _____
   _____

56 | ◯ = too easy | ☐ = too hard | △ = just right |

Skill: Predicting consequences and conclusions

Name _____

Write three or four sentences to explain
what will happen next.

1. An orthodontist prescribes expensive braces.

_____
_____
_____
_____
_____

2. You sleep too late, missing an interview for a job you really wanted.

_____
_____
_____
_____
_____

3. A thief asks you to hide some stolen money.

_____
_____
_____
_____
_____

| ◯ = too easy | ▢ = too hard | △ = just right | **57** |

Name _____

Write three or four sentences to explain
what will happen next.

1. You buy an expensive gift for your friend. The next day in school, you see
    that your friend has the exact item you are about to give.

    _____
    _____
    _____
    _____
    _____

2. You spent all evening doing your homework, but you left the papers at
    home. Now your teacher, who hates excuses, is collecting students'
    homework.

    _____
    _____
    _____
    _____
    _____

3. You win a national prize for an essay you did not write.

    _____
    _____
    _____
    _____
    _____

58

| ◯ = too easy | ☐ = too hard | △ = just right |

Skill: Predicting consequences and conclusions

Answer Key

Page 7

The following words should be underlined (accept reasonable variations):

1. as soon as the first cake was eaten, 2. as she graded the reports, 3. soon, 4. During our practice, 5. At last, 6. By the next summer, 7. Every now and then, 8. Long ago, 9. Early the next morning, 10. hundreds of years ago, 11. In the winter, 12. By the end of the day.

Page 8

The following words should be underlined (accept reasonable variations):

1. after school, 2. always, 3. before Columbus arrived in 1492, 4. every Wednesday, 5. then, 6. during the storm, 7. once in a while, 8. in a few months, 9. Next, 10. this morning, 11. When summer comes, 12. when everyone arrives.

Page 9

Accept reasonable variations of the following answers:

1. we traveled a long way, 2. we practiced for many hours, 3. we were dressed, 4. James bought the ingredients, 5. the class made a model city, 6. long cold winter, 7. Some children learn to read, 8. John needed braces, 9. Glenda enjoyed school, 10. The best team won the game.

Page 10

Accept reasonable variations of the following answers:

1. Janice bought her tickets, 2. We learned to draw well, 3. Amanda finally opened the package, 4. they were lucky to find a motel, 5. Jim got into trouble, 6. Dick is happy, 7. the blaze was out, 8. he drinks water three times a day, 9. the sky cleared by morning, 10. we picnicked near the monument.

Page 11

Accept appropriate responses.

Page 12

Accept appropriate responses.

Page 13

Accept appropriate adjectives.

Page 14

Accept appropriate adjectives.

Page 15

Accept appropriate adjectives.

Page 16
Accept appropriate adjectives and adverbs.

Page 17
Accept appropriate responses.

Page 18
Accept appropriate responses that indicate how.

Page 19
Accept appropriate responses.

Page 20
Accept appropriate responses.

Page 21
The following words should be circled:
1. adept, 2. teammate, 3. admirable, 4. despise, 5. lose, 6. rigid, 7. indifference, 8. scared, 9. following, 10. inattentive, 11. discard, 12. unprepared, 13. rare, 14. contract, 15. expense, 16. cowardice, 17. costly, 18. flourish, 19. convinced, 20. deep.

Page 22
Accept appropriate antonyms.

Page 23
The following words should be circled:
1. repair, 2. rule, 3. conceited, 4. comply, 5. ignore, 6. tidy, 7. loud, 8. keep, 9. harsh, 10. regular, 11. decide, 12. option, 13. swift, 14. conscious, 15. shy, 16. annoy, 17. freedom, 18. love, 19. corrupt, 20. blend.

Page 24
Accept appropriate synonyms.

Page 25
Accept appropriate responses.

Page 26
Accept appropriate responses.

Page 27
Accept appropriate responses.

Page 28
Accept appropriate responses.

Page 29
Accept appropriate pictures and responses.

Page 30
Accept appropriate pictures and responses.

Page 31
Accept appropriate pictures and responses.

Page 32
Accept appropriate questions.

Page 33
Accept appropriate responses.

Page 34
Accept appropriate pictures.

Page 35
Accept appropriate pictures.

Page 36
Accept appropriate pictures.

Page 37
Accept appropriate pictures and responses.

Page 38
Accept appropriate pictures and responses.

Page 39
Accept appropriate pictures and responses.

Page 40
Accept appropriate responses.

Page 41
Accept appropriate responses.

Page 42
Accept appropriate questions.

Page 43
Accept appropriate questions.

Page 44
Accept appropriate responses.

Page 45
Accept appropriate responses.

Page 46
Accept appropriate pictures and responses.

Page 47
Accept appropriate pictures and responses.

Page 48
Accept appropriate pictures and responses.

Page 49
Accept appropriate pictures and responses.

Page 50
Accept appropriate pictures and responses.

Page 51
Accept appropriate responses.

Page 52
Accept appropriate responses.

Page 53
Accept appropriate responses.

Page 54
Accept appropriate responses.

Page 55
Accept appropriate responses.

Page 56
Accept appropriate responses.

Page 57
Accept appropriate responses.

Page 58
Accept appropriate responses.